HUMAN BEHAVIOR OR TECHNOLOGY MAY IMPROVE ECONOMIC

DEVELOPMENT

JOHN LOK

Contents

Preface

Introduction

What methods may help human to create clever as well as creative ability? Human behavior or technology may help economic development? I shall indicate robot technology invention how to train human creative ability , also I shall explain whether robot tool may help human to improve economy development or help businessmen to reduce cost. Readers can make analysis whether robots may help human to bring long term economic benefits and improve ourselves ability and reduce cost for businesses.

Prologue

Content of content

Chapter 1 Can training brain art ability improve economy

What does brain art creative ability mean p.2-10
Learning brain art creative ability skills p.11-15
Chapter 2 Training brains creative effort economic methods
The relationship between enough sleeping and
brain imagination art creative ability raising level
p.16-20

What the methods to train brain creative effort?
p.21-25

Chapter 3 Can exercise improve brain ability to develop economy

Why do frequent brain creative imagination exercise, they may help ourslevs brains to raise brain creative effort more easily or effectively?
p.26-31

Psychological methods raise brain art imagination creative effort
Can habit leisure hobbies bring more brain imagination effort p.32-36
Training and teaching methods raise brain imagination creative effort in possibility p.37-42

Chapter 4 Can improve IQ ability to influence economy
Improvement IQ raises brain art imagination creative effort development p.43-50

Creative drawing paint effort brain development p.51-55
Improving brain creative effort future development p.56-60

Chapter 5
Technology or human behavior whether may influence economic growth or recession

Human Behavioral network job brings social
economic benefits
    What does human network job mean
    Why human network job behavior may influence economy p.61-80

Robots take our jobs behavioral and economy influences
    Robot job behavior brings economy influences

Intellectual human economic behaviors
What does intellectual human economic behaviors
mean ?
    The relationship between social change and human
behavior
    How human productive behavior may influence economic development
p.81-100
● New Zealand farmer individual wine productive behavior
● America high technological productive behavior
● China share market investing behavior
Why has any individual country have many people invest share behavior
which can influence the country's macro consumption desire?
Can technology influence human shopping behavioral change?
    Why and how human behavior may influence the country's economic
growth or recession?
Technology how impacts human behavior changing?
How and why employees behaviors may influence economy development?
Robots invention whether they can help organizations to raise efficiencies
or inefficiencies?
Why social behavior may influence organizational strategy needs to be
changed ?
Reasons why human behavior may influence economic recession or growth
?
How employee behavior influences organizational development?
Artificial intelligent Human clever and art creating ability methods
Why does technology raise online products sale demand and reduces shops
products sale demand?
Does car technological development reach mature stage to help economic
development?

PROLOGUE

CHAPTER ONE

Can training brain art ability improve economy

What does brain imagination art creative ability mean ?

Can we train ourselves brains to raise more art creative abilities? One excellent author, painter, music writer, clothing designer, house designer, dance performer etc. different kinds of art creative performers, whether they use some methods or skills to raise their brain imagination art creative effort or it is themselves owning genius brain imagination art creative abilities from their born or birth date.

It is one interesting question concerns how to raise ourselves brain imagination art creative efforts. Firstly, we need to know whether what brain imagination art creative effort means. In fact, many people feel some art genius, their imagination art creative abilities are due to their parents give them. It means that when they born, they must be genius, any kinds of art imagination creative efforts that they must own, e.g. some genius own writing story creative content ability, creating song or music ability, creative beautiful paints ability, designing clothes or houses or any things ability, creative dance performance ability.

However, some brain scientists or brain doctors or psychologists explain that evidences and experiments indicate may of art geniuses, their art imagination creative abilities are due to their learning more than themselves born to own from parents.

What does brain imagination creative effort mean? Brain imaginations art creative abilities may include many kinds of brain creating imaginations. For musical imaginations example, it may explain any creative aspects of music listening in the activities of composition, improvisation, and performance. So, the music or song writer can own good brain of music creative effort to write many different nature of musical beauty to bring enjoying and listening song or music emotion to music or song listeners.

So, brain imagination may include music or song creativity to any one. But, the differences between good music or bad music creativity may due to the music or song creativity may due to the music or song imagination creator whether who owns what level of musical knowledge, training, literacy, writing music or song experience, or playing music performance experience to the music listener individual listening music or song taste etc. different factors to bring individual emotion response to feel whether the song or music is good or bad after the music writer finished to write the song.

So, any kinds of song or music creativities have close relationship to the creator's brain music or song imagination creating effort had how much. It means that of the music creator owns high level of brain music imagination creative effort, then the music creator ought have enough effort to create many good song or good music to let any one listener to listen and feel their song or music creativities can own unique listening feeling to compare general music creators their common music or song creativities.

On theory explanation, brain imagination may mean that creative thinking, creating thinking is defined as the competence to engage any kinds of brain imagination productively in the generation, evaluation, and improvement of anyone of brain imagination, ideas, that can result in original and effective solutions, advances in any kinds of knowledge imagination , e.g. design a house, design a cloth, design a product, writing one story, writing one music or song, design a dance performance, painting a picture etc. different kinds of imagination.

Imagination may be listening imagination, e.g. song, music or reading a story book, wearing a dressing cloth, living a house, seeing a dance performance. Hence, imagination may be touched or seen or felt by any one. Hence, any one creative art performer must need have excellent creative thinking to create their product imagination, e.g. how to write one good story, how to write a good listening song, how to design a house or a cloth or a product, how to prepare a dancer performance etc. different kinds of creative product imagination to let any one customer to feel their creative products can have the unique or excellent quality to compare other general similar or same kinds of creative products.

Thus, imagination is the seed of creativity. Indeed, there is one fundamental skill that makes creativity possible. Without imagination, there can be no creativity. Imagination refers broadly to the human capacity to construct a mental representation of the which is nor currently present to the senses (Markman, Klein, & Suhr, 2009; Seligman et al., 2016).

Across social –emotional domains, there are a number of forms of imaginative thought, include thinking informed by an understanding of multiple cultures, pretend play, prospection, memory construction, counterfactual thinking, and mind wandering (Abraham, 2016 ; Runce & Pina, 2013). Many forms of imagination, specially imagination about people, including oneself, across time and space, draw heavily on the brain's default mode network, a network composed of several brain regions along the midline of the medial prefrontal cortex, medial pertietal cortex (Andrews, Hanna, Smallwood & Spreng, 2014; Zmmordion-Yang Christodoulour, & Singh 2012, Raichle & Snyder, 2007, Schactot, Addis & Buckner, 2007). Other forms of imagination that involve visualizing, physical objects or physical space are thought to recruit more heavily the brain's executive attention network and dorsal attention network, a network involving communication between the frontal eye fields and the intreperietal succs (Andres- Hanna et al., 2014: Jack et al 2013).

Hence, many brain doctors and brain scientists and psychologists imply that imagination is the seed of creativity. Genius's unique creativities can be caused by their brain imagination. Any one creative product creator whose brain may be trained to own unique creative effort by themselves learning or nay new creative knowledge skills or methods in order to achieve to raise themselves brain imagination creative efforts.

On conclusion, it seems that why any one creative effort is due to creator whose imagination creative effort is due to they attempt to learn new creative knowledge more than their born genius to own creative effort. Many brain doctors or brain scientists or psychologists began to research how to raise ourselves brains to achieve owning excellent imagination creative effort. I shall attempt to explain how we can attempt to learn in order to raise ourselves brains imagination creative efforts in order to become one excellent painter, music/song writer, author, designer, dance performer etc. different kinds of creative occupation performers.

CHAPTER TWO

Training brains creative effort economic methods

Can we apply some methods or skills to help ourselves brains to raise imagination creative effort? In fact, many brain doctors or brain scientists or psychologists began to research whether we can apply what skills to improve ourselves brains imagination creative efforts. They had began to attempt to find any one to attempt to do any brain imagination improvement experiments . Their aims to find the best skills to help human to improve brain imagination memory in order to create high level art performers. If one day, human individual brain can be trained to raise brain imagination memory function effort, then many general level of authors, painters, music or song writers , art performers, designers , their skills can be improved to be one proficient art work creator easily. Because if they can be confirmed that one kind skill or some skills can help themselves brains to raise imagination creating effort significantly. Then, when every common art work creator occupation performer can learn any useful skills to attempt to raise their brain imagination creative effort, it can bring much benefits to our societies because when many common art creative performers can confirm to improve their brain imagination creative effort from some skillful trainings. Consequently, we will have much beautiful cloths to wear, good design of houses to live , good music or song to listen, see beautiful drawing pictures, good books to read , good dance performances to see, because all of these creative art performers, their imagination creating effort can be improved significantly. Then , our social cultural level will be influence to raise in long time significantly.

The question concerns whether what skills or methods may help ourselves brains to raise imagination creative efforts? I shall attempt to indicate some possible skills or methods, they may help ourselves brains to raise imagination creative efforts as below:

For dancer performance behavior example, it is at its simplest, allowing your child to thrive though constant play and exploration, uninhibited by the strict rules of science, reason, law or a judgmental society. For any one dancer, it requires an open channel to allow dancer behavioral information and ideas to flow freely into the dancer's space. It requires an open mind and a sense of freedom and limitlessness. So, one proficient dancer needs to own high dance skillful memory to remember every whose dance behavior as well as learn how to create good dance skills in order to attract audiences attention and satisfy their visual dance enjoyment feeling on the theatre hall.

Hence, dancer needs to raise whose dance skillful imagination creative effort, it means that they need to learn how to excite themselves brains to create dance behavioral imagination in order to improve themselves dance skills effectively.

I believe that strongly in the idea of every human action stemming from a complex environmental factors. I also believe an extra ingredient is somehow part of imagination. An internal imaginal word, so such as one proficient dancer case, if she can train herself brain to remember every high level dance steps easily. Then, she ought improve herself dance skills in short time rapidly. So, training to remember dance steps , which is needed to help the common dancer to become one proficient dancer more easily. For dancer case, she may use imagination to recall emotions needed in interpreting a character for any one dance performance to picture an overall aesthetic before it comes to fruition, to invent new artistic dance concepts, to invent new movements to connect old movements , to picture the dancer whose body executing a movement before she has even done the dance steps, to try something new dance steps. Hence, new dance steps and dance bogy behaviors from whose old dance st4eps and body dancing behaviors in order to achieve to feel her dance steps and body dancing behaviors had been improved significantly. It is one good skill to improve anyo0ne common dancer dancing skills, when she can train herself brain to create good dancing steps and dancing body behaviors as well as remember every old dancing body behavior or dancing steps in order to raise how to improve or create new dancing body behavior or new dancing steps. Consequently, she can learn how to change new dancing body behaviors in order to improve herself old dancing skill easily. Hence, any one dancer must need to raise whose brain dance imagination creative effort in order to improve whose old dance skills significantly.

Research concerning the role of memory in imagination or brain imagination creative effort skill issue, it is future interesting brain behavioral research issue for any one brain doctor or brain scientist or psychologist. They aim to help our societies to produce more excellent art creative performers. Most psychological theories of imagination can be seen as theories of imagination consider that " creative" imagination, e.g. paint, writing a story, playing music, designing a house, designing a cloth, designing a dancing steps. All of any these, they belong to " creative imagination". Their imagination is needed to create by ourselves brains. When ourselves brains have clear picture, then the author can follow his brain picture or mind to create a story content, write a song, design a house or a cloth or organize a dancing steps.

Hence, " brain imagination picture" may be one main element to help any one creative performer to create any kinds of creative product very easily. If the creative performer can own good brain picture memory, then his story content can be more attraction, his dancing steps can be more attraction, his house or cloth or any kinds of products design can be more attraction. The question concerns how to create attractive brain picture imagination? Hence, when the art creative performer can have good brain imagination, then he/she ought have good creativity or creative effort in order to create whose new story , new song, new design house of cloth or new dancing steps very easily.

`In fact, imagination pervades human experience. Children begin engaging in pretend play and although cultural and parental attitudes affect the amount and content of imagination play. As adults, we are consumers and creators of fiction, song, story, house, designer, dance performance etc. and we respond emotionally to imagined scenarios. Moreover, we invent fictions even in the pursuit of facts, face of neurological disorders, in defending the bases of our decisions, and in the construction of autobiographical memory.

However, by applying useful knowledge in extraordinary events with heightened emotional content, learners may be better able to access important cultural skills or facts. Consistent with this, researchers have suggested that imaginative engagement might support a range of cognitive abilities, including creativity, intelligences, problem solving, symbolic reasoning, language development , theory of mind, narrative skills, social skills, causal reasoning , emotional regulation , and executive function.

I believe that thinking of new ideas is not an optional exercise in creativity. It is fundamental to learning . The learner must need gather new information in order to raise whose brain imagination creative effort. So, gathering new information is the best method to help our brains to raise imagination creative effort. It is more effective to compare how to think of new ideas to achieve how to create ourselves brain imagination creative effort. For a dancer, if she can attempt to gather any new dancing styles new information from internet channel daily. I believe that she can improve whose dancing steps in order to create new dance style more easily. Otherwise, if she only concentrates on how to think her new dance style ideas by herself mind. I believe that she can not create any new dance attractive style to improve her old poor dancing style easily. Hence, gathering new information may be another useful brain imagination creative effort improvement skill.

Another kind of method is that teaching anyone to new skill. One of the best ways to expand your learning is to teach a skill to another person. After you learn a new skill, you need to practice it. Teaching a new skill to others needs you to explain the concept and correct any mistakes you make. This can improve your mental activeness to a great extent. Next method is that spending spare time for physical activity, many studies have confirmed that daily physical activity also keeps the brain sharp and active. The simple science behi8nd this is that physical activity accelerates the circulation of oxygen on the mind. All of these methods can help your brains to improve memory and raise brain imaginatio0n creative effort effectively. Then, we can improve memory, it can assist us to raise creative thinking or creativity.

Creativity means the ability to change traditional ideas, rules, patterns, relationships and to create meaningful new ideas, forms, methods etc. originality, progressiveness, or imagination. In fact, every one has the capacity to be creative. In the psychological view, these is a debate over whether anyone is born with innate creativity or if everyone who has it has developed a talent. Though some scientists believe certain individuals have a higher aptitude for creativity, many attest that creativity is an actually a skill and anyone can learn a skill. This is the integration of memory and creative thinking at work.

Consequently, we tend to think a parts of the brain specialized for one thing, one particular function at a time. However, neuroscentists attest that all parts of the brain are constantly interacting and building strong neural pathways is the best way to keep all parts of the brain healthy. Finally, I shall indicate ways to exercise creative thinking skills, e.g. changing your routine, you will need to experience anything new or give yourself a new experience to active your brain in creative process. Try changing something small or adding a new activity each day. Thus will help your brain and your body to stretch your creative muscles, or read a book or listen music, anyone of these daily habit behaviors, they will help your brains to raise imagination creative effort effectively. Hence, we can not neglect any one of these simple skills or living habits, they may help ourselves brains to raise imagination creative effort indeed.

CHAPTER THREE

Can exercise improve brain ability to develop economy

The relationship between enough sleeping and
brain imagination art creative ability raising level

Can keeping enough sleeping time raise brain creative imagination effort or raise memory? Can enough sleeping influence our brains own more art creative ability, e.g. creating good story content ability, drawing beautiful paint image ability, creat5ing good song or music ability, creating beautiful house or cloth or any kinds of products ability? Many brain scientists had begun to research how enough sleeping time has direct or indirect relationship to improve ourselves brains creative efforts. They also believe that it is possible that enough sleeping time may help ourselves brains to improve creative e and memory effort. If it is true, whether we need to sleep how many hours in order to improve ourselves brains creative efforts. Otherwise, if we lack enough sleeping time, our brains creative e efforts will be influenced to poor? For example, one owning many years writing experience proficient author, if he can not have enough sleeping time every day, it can bring poor creative story imagination mind ability to recreate any new story content in possible. It is one interesting question concerns the relationship between enough sleeping time and brain creative ability research? I shall attempt to indicate evidences to explain their relationship as below:

` Any one must need sleep. If one lacks at least 8 hours sleeping time in the day, he won't have enough nervous to do any matters, even jobs. So , it seems that any creative tasks, e.g. writing stories, painting pictures, designing houses, cloths etc. creative jobs. The art creator must need have enough time to sleep in order to prepare to raise his brain imagination creative feeling to achieve how to design one beautiful house in order to attract people to choose this house to buy in preference, or design one beautiful cloth to attract people to choose his design cloth to wear in preference, how to write horror story content to let readers to feel fear or write romance story content to let readers to feel they are lovers both or write space scientific story content to let readers to feel that they are catching rocket to fly to outer strange space environment to carry on one time space existing journey, even how to design one time attractive dance performance to let audiences to feel all dancers to feel all dancers are performing attractive dance steps or create soft music to let music listeners to feel this music is soft or comfortable to listen, when they are sitting in the theatre to listen this music performance. So, all of these creative tasks to the art creator, who must need have clear brain imagination or nervous to help them to create any one of those creative product in order to let customers or audiences feel their creative products are beautiful or attractive to compare other some creators whose art products.

Hence, art creative imagination must need to any one art creator, if he/she hopes that his/her art creative product can bring more attraction to any one art product buyers or audience to consider more to compare his/her other same art creative product competitors. So, any one art creator must not need to own high educational level of working experiences . Otherwise, they must need top own high level art imagination ability to compare general people. Hence, it is true that any one art creator must need have more clear and good imagination effort to compare other occupation working people in our societies, if they hope to own good creative imagination effort to attempt to create their any kinds of creative products, e.g. design of a house, a cloth, write one story etc. creative products. So, it is ensure that creative art product ought need have good brain imaginatio0n to compare general occupations.

In fact, many brain scientists or brain doctors or psychologists believe that enough sleeping time, it can influence any one whose nervous next day, such as they had attempted to carry on many brain imagination creative effort researches or experiments . They confirm that if the art product creator or art entertainer can have enough sleeping time, it can help the art product creator or art entertainer to create good dance performance, good listening soft music, one beautiful design house or cloth , dancing a good dance performance to compare lacking enough sleeping time product creator or art entertainer. Hence, it seems that enough sleeping time may assist any one art creator to raise brain imagination creative effort.

What the methods to train brain creative effort?

How we can train ourselves brains to raise high creative efforts? Can we train ourselves brains creative efforts by learning method? Has it close relationshipship between ourselves bpdies and ourselves brain creative efforts? Do ourselves brains creative efforts to be poor if we have no health bodies?

I believe that we must need have health bodies, then our health bodies may bring more creative effort to ourselves brains easily, because health bodies may help us to raise ,memory ability, keeping happy and pleasure positive emotin to do any things every day. Due to our brains must be our part of bodies. Our brains are inside to our bodies. Although, we can not see our brains , but we can feel oursleves brains are working, if our memory is high, e.g. we can remember our teachers what they had taught all contents after every lesson. Then, our examination results must be improved because we have good memory . So, enough sleeping time is one good method to raise ourselves brains' memories.

In fact, enough sleeping time does not needed to have enough training. So, training our brains to raise creative effort method, we only need have enough sleeping time in order to keep our brains have enough nervous to remember any thibgs more easily, e.g. studying is one good example for remembering training action or behavior, we can attempt to train ourselves brains to remember any new knowledge from teacher individual teaching. When we learn any new knowledge in lessons, we are using ourselves brains to attrmpt to remember what the teacher is teaching in lesson . If we brains feel tried, we can have breaking time for less sleeping time between lessons in order to keep ourselves brain memory longer time.

In fact, ourselves brains memory and brains creative effort whether they are high or low level, they have close relationship because our creative effort may be influenced to raise if our memory effort can increase rapidly and it can be kept longer time. Many brain doctors, psychologists, brain scientists had researched to attempt to do experiments to confirm that brain creative effort and brain memory effort have close relationship. Hence, many of them begin to believe that if one person can have high memory effort, then whose brain ought have hifh creative effort, e.g. creative story writing ability, creative drawing paint ability, creative music or song ability, creative designing house, or cloth or any products abiliity . All of these different kinds of brain creative abilities , they must have absolute relationship to brain memory. It means that if your brain can have good memory ability to remember or learn any kinds of new knowledge rapidly in long time, then your brain can have high creative ability to be trained to create any kinds of new knowledge easily, e.g. writing fun story, writing fun or good listening song or music, drawing beautiful paint, design attraction of house or cloth etc. any products, even organizing good dance performance. All of these creative tasks must need have good memory ability to the creator, hence, enough sleeping time must be the best method to help us to improve oursleves brain memory or brain creative effort both. We can not neglect to keep enough sleeping time in order to raise oursleves brain memory and creative effort both, if we hope to become an excellent story writer, music or song writer, house or cloth design, good organized performance dancer.

On conclusion, attempting to apply brain memory effort to do creative effort skillful tasks, when one person can have enough sleeping time every day, then his brain memory ability may be influenced to raise or improve. He can attempt to do some simple creative task, e.g. learning how to draw one natural environment scene paint, learning hoe to create a horror story, learning how to create a good listening song or music, even learning how to organize every steps for the dance performance etc. different kinds of creative tasks behaviors. Because when the person feels that he has enough sleeping time, his memory ability may be influenced to increase memory ability. When one house designer, he feels that his memory ability is increasing, he ought remember all prior beautiful or urgue house design in his memory if he is one house designer. After this house designer's prior all house design drawing picture will be remembered again. So, this house designer can remember all his poor drawing paints in order to improve or understand whether how he ought continue to draw or improve his new house picture in order to design his new house design more easily. Because when one house designe needs to spend time to create or design one new house. If he can remember which kinds of house , he had drawn in past in his brain memory. Then, he can avoid to repeat to design his past old house design again. He can use his new house design method to create another new house paint design. So, this house designer can improve his new house paint design if he can remember what kinds of houses, he had painted to design in his past. Then, he can avodi to repeat to design the kind of similar or same style of house again. Consequently, one good brain memory house designer can avoid to design same or similar house again, then this house deisgn may have more house design creative effort in order to design his next new house easily. So, it explains why it may have close relationship between brain memory and brain creative effort.

Can exercise bring more creative effort to brains

Any excellent occupation people who must need to often do exercises in order to achieve excellent performance, such as sportman, doctor, lawyer, accountant, engineer, teacher, architect, singer etc. different professional occupations. All of these occupation people, who must need to spend time to do exercises repeatly again in order to achieve proficent performance or proficent skills. The question concerns whether of one creative art working person who often do exercise, then he/she can bring more creative effort to themselves brains, e.g. one authoer often does imagination to feel new things in order to attempt to write any new story. In his/she creative imagination process, whether himself/herself brain can be influenced to raise or improve or increase effort when he/she often uses his/her brain to mind any new science story scene to achieve brain creative effort or if one musican often uses himself/herself brain to attempt to mind any new music suddenly. When he/she feels himself/herself brain has one good music or song suddenly, then he/she writes down the music or song in order to avoid that he/she forgets when himself/herself brian has this new music or song imagination in his/her mind. So, he / she often does music /song creative exercise in order to improve his/her any new music/song imagination. Can this musician often do music/song creative imagination to bring high brain creative level? For a house deisgner example, if this house deisgner often does brain creative exercise to draw any house design or house picture when he /she feels himself/herself brain has any unique house imagination suddenly. Can his/her frequent drawing any new house picture design behavior, which changes hisself/herself brain creative effort to be raised significantly? So, such as my explanation that it is possible that any exploration that it is possible that any person can attempt to do brain creative exercise in order to raiee our brain creative effort more significantly and easily.

Why do frequent brain creative imagination exercise, they may help oursleves brains to raise brain creative effort more easily or effectively? I shall attempt to explain as below:

Our brains are similar to our bodies, e.g. hand, foot. We must need often do exercises, in order to let we can run rapidly or climb mountains safely or we can swim rapidly. So, if one sportman hopes to win the sport competition, he/she will often run or swim or climb mountains or ride bicycles before this sport competition will begin. So, our brains are such as our part of bodies. Ourselves brains must often need to be done exercises in order to raise creative effort, if we hope tobecome one proficient creative author, drawing painter, house designer, cloth designer , musician etc. art creators.

Our brains must be needed to do any creative mind exercises again and again every day in order to improve oursleves brains imagination creative effort significantly. Any one proficient art creator, who must not be talent especially, they must not own unique talent characteristics. Otherwise, some of talent art creator , e.g. author, musician, house or cloth designer, painter et.c they may be foolish people in general. But, if they can often keepto do brain creative exercises, when they feel any new things in themslves mind suddenly, e.g. one special house picture imagination, one special beautiful cloth picture imagination, one good listening song or music imagination or mind. They can write down to record on paper immediately. If they can keep to write on paper to record any new picture imagination in habit. Their brain creative imagination exercise behaviors, which can help them to train their brains to learn how to create new imagination picture skills, e.g. let them to feel to create any new music or song easily, let them to feel to draw or design any house or cloth imagination easily, let them to feel to create any new story content easily, let them to feel to organize one unique dance performance easily.

What factor may cause any one of above art creator to feel how to create any new creative product easily? The main factor is that " exercise" , due to they can often train their brains to learn how to attempt to create new story content, new music or song , new house or cloth design, new dance performance stepping. When they often use themselves brains to create any new creative products, and write down on paper or draw on paper in order to record their any new creative products as well as aovid to forget their any new creative products. Then, they can revise their past creative products in order to improve their past creative products to be better.

In their " brain creative process exercises", they must help any one of these art creators to raise themselves brain creative effort significantly. Hence, " brain art creative exercise" may be one good method to help any one art creator to raise their art creative skills.

Psychological methods raise brain art imagination creative effort

Can habit leisure hobbies bring more brain imagination effort

How to learn effort in order to raise more brain imagination? Can learning bring more brain imagination effort? For example, if one person often needs any another person writing stories, in his/her reading process can it raise his/her writing ability? If one person often listens music or song , in his/her listening music or song process, can it raise his/her writing music or song creative ability? If one person often watching horror movies, in his/her watching horroe movies pricess, can it raise his/her creating horror movie imagination effort? If one person often sees cloth magazine photos, in his /her seeing cloth photos process, can it raise his/her design cloth creative effort? If one person often sees house magazine photos, can it raise his/her design house effort? If one person often sees dance performance, in his/her seeing dance performance process, can it raise his/ her organise dance performance effort? If one person often sees paints, in his /her seeing paint process, can it raise his/her drawing paint brain art creative process?

Some brain doctors, brain scientists, psychologists begain to research whether if general people often to read books, listen music/songs, see movies, see house or cloth magazines, see dance performance, see paints etc. different hobbies, when whose these different kinds of hobbies become leisure behaviors, whether their these different kinds of leisure behaviors can influence themselves brains raise imagination creative efforts. Some brain doctors or brain scientists had confirmed that when general people can spend about 2 to 3 hours per day to read stories, listen music/song, see movie, read cloth or house photo magazine, see paints, see dance performances etc. different kinds of hobbies or lesiure behaviors. Then, these general people whose brains can be influenced to raise more imagaination creative efforts, .e.g. creating story content effort, creating music or song effort, designing house or cloth effort, organizing dance performance effort, creating movie content effort, creating paint picture effort, because when general individual can spend time to do any one of these leisure actions to be habit bobbies every day. Although , they do not be trained or taught from teachers, or they do not born to own high creative effort, but when general individual can attempt to spend time to feel enjoyable to choose to do any one of these leisure action to become hobbies. Then, their brains may be influences to raise writing story, writing music/song, drawing paint, organizing dance performance, design house or cloth etc. different aspects of art creative efforts.

On conclusion, when one general individual can often spend time to do leisure actions or behaviors to be hobbies, then they may help themselves to raise brain imagination creative effort in possible. So, we can attempt to choose any kinds of leisure interest to be leisure hobbies as well as do leisure actions in habit, then our leisure habits will help oursleves brains to raise art creative efforts in possible.

Training and teaching methods raise brain imagination creative effort in possibility

Can general people be trained or be taught in order to help ourselves brains to raise imagination creative efforts? Many brain scientists and brain doctors had began to find general people to do experiments concern whether any general people whose brain imagination effort can be influenced to raise after they are taught or are trained, e.g. learning drawing paint skills, learning dance skills, learning creative story content skills, learning house or cloth or product design skills etc. different kinds of imagination behaviors. However, they discovered that although any one can learn general writing story, writing music or song , design house, cloth or any kinds of products skills, draw paint, or organize dance performance etc. art creative skills, but it does not represent that their brains can be influenced to raise imagination creative effort. The reason is that it is different between raising creative brain effort and raising creative skills effort.

In general, we can learn general writing book, writing music or song, designing house or cloth or any kinds of products, drawing paints, dancing etc. art creative skills or art creative methos by teaching or training methods. So, art teacher may let us to learn any kinds of art creative skills, but, if we hope to raise or improve ourselves brain art creative effort. It is not possible that teaching and training methods both may hepp us to raise brain art creative effort, because human brain is one part of ourselves bodies. Brain is not hand or foot, we can use hand and foot to attempt to do any art creative tasks, e.g. how to use hand to draw one beautiful paint, hoe to use foot to dance, how to use hand to design one beautiful house or cloth or any kinds of products. So, learning art creative skills, it means that learning how to use hand or foot to do any art creative behaviors. We can only learn art creative skills hoe to use hand to draw beautiful paint, how to use foot to dance, how to hand to design one house, one cloth or any kinds of products. So, teaching and training methods can only let us to learn how to use hand or foot to do art creative skillful behavior more easily. These both methods can not help ourselves brains to raise brain art imagination creative effort in possible.

Nowadays, many brain scientists and brain doctors began to believe that teaching and training both methods only help oursleves to learn how to use hands to improve drawing paints behaviors in order to achieve more easily or how to use foots to improve dancing behaviors in order to achieve more attractive dance performance or how to design cloth or house or any kinds of products more attraction, or how to use our mouths to sing more attraction of sonds. All of above these art creative behaviors are only " art creative skills". When we are taught or trained to learn any one of these art creative skills by teachers, ourselves brains won's be influenced to raise any kinds of art creative efforts. So, teaching and training both methods can not raise ourselves brains creative effort. Otherwise, these both methods may only help ourselves hands and foots to improve art creative skillful behaviors in order to achieve how to use hands to draw paints more easily, how to write story content more attraction, how ro use hands to design house or cloth or any kinds of products more attraction, how to use our mouths to sing songs more clearly. If we hope to improve or raise ourselves brains art creative efforts to be any kinds of art creator, we can only keep enough sleeping time every day, keeping habits to read books, keeping habits to see any cloth or house magazines, keeping habits to listen any kinds of music, or see any dance performance etc. different kinds of art leisure activities, because when we can enjoy to do any kinds of art creative leisures when we spend nervous to do these leisure activities in habit. Then, ourselves brains can be excited to raise any kinds of art excited to raise any kinds of arr imagination creative efforts by other artists. Consequently, ourselves brains art creative minds may be influenced to improve , even raise brain art creative effort , due to ourselves brains had saved more different artists whose art imagination of memories.

CHAPTER FOUR

Can improve IQ ability to influence economy

Improvement IQ raises brain art imagination creative effort development

Can we improve ourselves IQ in order to raise ourselves brain imagination creative effort? Do IQ and brain imagination, chich has cause and effect close relationship?
Nowadays, many brain scientists and brain doctors began to attempt to find young people to do experiments to research whether their brain art imagination creative effort cab ne raised if
their IQ can be trained to improve their mind analysis and logic judgement effort. In results, they conclude unique conclusions, their investigations discover that if one young person whose IQ can be trained to climb up to above 100 marks, then their mind and analysis and logic judgement effort may be influenced to raise, even their brain art imagination creative effort may also be influenced to improve in possible. Hence, many of brain doctors or brain scientists or psychologists begin to believe that training on IQ improvement method can bring positive art imagination creative effort influences to develop our brain's mind analysis, ligic, judgement efforts. So, if one person , he/she can be trained to improve his/her IQ mind effort from his/her child age stage till to adult age stage. Consequently, his/her brain art imagination creative effort may be raised to more 50% of his/her general brain art imagination creative effort level.

It brings this question: WHy can improve brain IQ level to influence oursleves grain art imagination creative effort to be raised? The answer is simple that I assume the one young owns
high IQ level, his/her mind analysis and logic judgement effort must be better than general low IQ level people. SO, when he/she owns high level

of mind analysis and logic judgement effort. He/she can spend less time to make more accurate judgement to solve any challenges, because his/her mind analysis and logic judgement effort compares to general low IQ level people is higher. So, when the young can be trained to reach high IQ level intelligent young, he/she can make much accurate mind analysis, logic judgement effort to know how to draw paints or pictures to let many audiences feel more beautiful to his/her creative pictures, how to create horror story content to feel readers to feel, how to sing or create the song in order to let listeners to feel

enjoyable to listen the song, how to organize the dance steps in order to attract audiences to see the dance peformance, how to design the house in order to let the house buyers feel the house design is attraction, how to design the cloth in order to let the cloth buyers feel comfortable to wear the cloth etc. different art creative tasks. So, it seems that it has cause and effect relationhsip between'IQ

improvement and brain art creative effort improvement . Because when we born, we must not own high IQ level or high brain art creative effort level. We must need to spend long time

to learn or to be trained to improve ourselves brain IQ level or brain art creative effort. Due to ourselves brain IQ level and brain art creative effort level will not be brought when we born in first day. I mean that we need time to be taught or be trained in order to improve ourselves brains IQ level or brain art creative effort level. Hence, IQ and art creative efforts have similar characteristics , such as intangible, feeling. So, we must need oursleves brains can be trained to bring high IQ level in order to improve oursleves brains art creative effort in possible. ON conclusion, improvement IQ level can be one kind of good method to help ourselves brains to improve art creative efforts significantly.

Creative drawing paint effort brain development

A painter hopes to learn how to use hands to draw any kinds of beautiful paints. INstead of colour choice, paint pen choice, painting drawing quality of paper choice, painting tools factor.

Can the painter himself/herself brain mind creative effort influence his/her paints pictures which they can attract audiences to feel himself/herself paints are beautiful to compare general painters. IN fact, drawing paint quality of papers, painting pens, colour quality of these painting tools factors may influence the picture is beautiful or attractive or not, but we can not

negligent that the painters whose brain mind creative effort also may influence their any one paint creative feeling. For exmaple, if the painter's brain can have good creative house effort, then his/her any house design will attract more people like to see his/her any house design picture to compare other house designers. Hence, this painter ought concentrate on attempting to design any kinds

of house pictures order to improve his/her any kinds of house design picture, due to his/her brain owns high mind creative effort to create any kinds of house to draw more easily to compare

other kinds of things. So, if he/she forgets to continue to draw any kinds of house pictures, then he/she chooses to draw natural scence or human face or human body or any things, such as cloth,furniture etc. paint pictures. I believe that this painter can not draw these kinds of pcitures to compare drawing house pictures more beautiful or attraction. Hence, it seems that an yone painter needs to know that whether the painter , his/her ability can draw which kinds of paint pictures more excellent or more proficient in order to concentrate on improving to draw this kind of paint pictures. Then, it brings this question: How doe this painter know that what kinds of painting pictures who can draw more proficient? The answer ensures be "what kinds of picture image, he/she can own more mind creative effort. Hence, the painter needs to know that what kinds of brain image that he can own more creative effort to draw the kind of image picture. For example, if one painter feels that he /she has more interest to draw any human face or body paint pictures as well as when he sees any one natural face or body, he can remember their body shape and face shape in his/her brain memory more clearly, even he /she also feel his/her owning human face or body image creative effort is more proficient or excellent more than to create any other kinds of things image to draw pictures. Them I   may ensure that painter ought concentrate on drawing any human faces or bodies picture images in order to improve his/her painting skills more eaisly. Hencem any painter must need to know whether which aspect of picture image himself or herself mind creative effort, that he/she ought own high brain image creative

effort on this kind of thing.

I mean that when the painter discovers that he /shw own high image creative effort on matural sene, he /she ought concentrate on drawing trees, flowers, woods, etc. natural environment pictures, or he /she discovers that owning high image creative effort on furnitures, bicycles, books, cups, toys etc. different kinds of productimages.Then. this painter ought concentrate on drawing any one of these products in prder to imrpve his/her drawing painting skills. Hence, any one painter must need to know whether he/she owns which aspect of brain

image creative effort in the highest level in order to draw his/her paint pictures more easily.

Improving brain creative effort future development

Nowadays, brain scientists, brain doctors, psychologists had began to research how to improve humans ourselves brains imagine creative effort significantly. They had began to apply robots to build brains which can similar to human brains, they had been carrying experiements to research whether future artificial brains can be invented to own general human's memory ability, even imagine creative ability. In fact, they had attempted to do robot brain scientific experiments, they concluded that it is possible that future robot (artificial intelligent) brains will have chance to invent to similar human's brain to learn mind , creativity, analysis, memory ability, even future robot (AI) brain development may be improved to exceed human's general memory, mind analysis, memory, even image creative effort level. Hence, it seems that future robots can be applied to do any kinds of art creative tasks. Moreover, (AI) robot brain art imagine creative ability, it is possible that their brain art imaginative efforts can be better that human ourselves brain e.g. creative effort.

Even, future human's brain art creative efforts can not attempt to exceed robot (AI)'s brain art creative efforts forever.

I assume that future brain scientists and robot (AI) brain scientists confirm that robots may be developed their brains own high level of mind, analysis, judgement, memory and art imagine creative efforts to compare human's ourselves brains development. Then, I bring these two questions: Can future robot replace human to do any art creative tasks ? Can robots and human art creative workers cooperate in order to bring better art creative products or robots or human art creative products or robots or human art creative workers work alone can bring better art creative products, due to robot art creative workers are human art creative workers' their art creative products occupation competitors. I shall attempt to answer above these both questions as below:

If brain scientists confirm that future robots (AI) themselves brains can be invented to achieve to own high level mind, analysis, memory, art creative effort, then, they ought to used to do any kinds of art creative tasks in our societies. For example, robots can be used to apply their image creative effort to help humans painters to apply art mind to judge how to draw any kinds of paints in order to raise the paint pictures' attraction ot robots can be used to apply their music or song creative effort to help human musicians to apply art mind to judge how to write one music or song in order to let listeners can feel soft music comfortable feeling or robots can be used to apply their image creative effort to help designer to judge how to design one cloth, one house, one magazine, book, advertisement cover or any kinds of products in order to attract buyers feel the kind of product design is more beautiful to achieve purchase in preference.

I assume that future robot (AI) brain art creative effort development ought be developed to exceed human ourselves general art creative effort in possible. Although, it must be good news if robots' brains art creative efforts may be improved to invent achieve to exceed human's brain general art creative efforts, but it also brings image bad news, they may influence many art image creative workers lose their art image creative workers lose their art image creative jobs when robots can be replaced to do any kinds of art replaced to do any kinds of art creative jobs in our future societies.

Have future our art creative tasks development must need to keep balance between robot's brains and human art creative workers' brains. I suggest that human art creative workers or performances ought not feel robots may be their main art creative occupational competitors. I mean that future any kinds of art creative workers ought cooperate with robots to do any kinds of art creative tasks together. So, robots' role is future any kinds of art creative workers' assistants for one painter example, he can apply robot's art imagine creative mind to help him to mind or analyzie how to draw the natural scene picture, e.g. how to use colour, how to drawing. pens to draw the natural scene picture to be improved , it aims to let audiences can feel more attraction. Hence, the painter may apply the robot's suggestion of natural scene picture to be picture image reference. Then the painter can observe the robot's finished natural scence picture to find whether what this natural scene picture weaknesses are, in order to revise whether how to improve this robot's designing natural scene picture its weaknesses to be strengths to attact audiences' observation or raise their visal comfortable feeling or visal satisfactory feeling to this natural scene picture.

Hence, future robot's roles are only any kinds of human art creative workers' assistants. They can only been given their any kinds of art creative products to let any one art creative workers to refer or revise in order to improve their creative skills from human art creative workers. So, I feel that they ought cooperate to create any kinds of art image creative pictures together to compare that they choose to do themsleves art creative tasks alone. When they can cooperate to work together , their any kinds of art creative products must be improved to increase attraction more easily.

Technology or human behavior whether may influence economic growth or recession

Human Behavioral network job brings social economic benefits

What does human network job mean ? Why may human network job be popular? Why human network job behavior may influence economy ? Nowadays internet is popular to use. We can apply internet to find data , search any new things, even earn money. Why does internet may become huma network job source. For example, e-publish may be one kind of new human network job. Any authors may apply internet channel to help them to sell electronic or paper books from e-publisher web store. They may apply facebook, you tub etc. any online channel to promote themselves new books to let new readers to know whether when they may buy themselves favourable new topic books to read

from electronic publisher web store.

Thus, future electronic publisher industry may help any authors to build internet network platform to help them to sell and promote ot advertise their any one new electronic or paper book topic to let global any one reader to choose to buy their any new topic books from electronic publisher web store easily and conveniently. However, it implies that electronic network platform author may be one kind of future new human network job in our societies.

How electronic network platform author job may bring economy benefit in macro economy view? A person can have few friends, contacts and still be very influential if these few

friends and contacts are themselves highly influential, e.g. one author must not need to know any one reader in global society. When they like to choose any electronic books from electronic internet network platform. They may become the author's any one topic book buyer, when they feel the author's any one topic book is fun and attract they make decision to buth the strange author whose the topic book from electronic book publisher's platform web store conventiently in short time. Although, they are strangers, they do not know themselves , but the reader can understand what it way that made Google from writing platofrm to create new creative mind and typing network job method to replace traditional hand writing book method for global authors. It will be one kind of new human network writing job.

Hence, global any one reader can apply an innovative search engine , such as google.com to find whether whom author personal new topic books are value to read from internet.

Then, the electroniuc publisher's web store may be new book store platform sale network to help the author to sell many electronic or paper books from electronic network platform

in short time. So, internet may be future new network plaform to help global any one author to create network writing job absolutely. Furthermore, internet may be popular social media

to help any one author to build goold relationship between his/her readers. It is one kind of new network, human network job. New authors do not need to buy many paper books to prepare to put in any one book shop warehouse. Their every book can print on demand to reduce out of book stock in any one book shop. They may choose to sell either electronic books or paper books both from any one book publisher web store. So, electronic network platform may be one kind of good writing channel to help human authors to create income and it can also help authors to bring new creative mind and new topic fun content books to let readers to know and buy to read from electronic publisher network platform.

Why does human behavior may be one kind of new human network job to bring global economic advantages. ALthough, it may be free income or without inocme, but the person does the network behavior, his/her behavior may be bring advantages to influence many other people's health. For this case, when a worker in a coffee shop in an airport gets a vaccination aganinst the flu, it does not only helps him or her stay healthy, but also helps the many travellers who might otherwise have been inflected if that workers caught the flu. So, the externality , the result implies the vaccination of even a part of a community conveys benefits to the whole community. For example, governments pay special attention to the vaccinations of school children, teachers, health mothers, and the elderly, categories of people particularly susceptible not only to catching, but also to transmitting a disease.

It is not accidental that governments are heavily involved with vaccination . When there are externalities, free market, fail to persuade individual incentives with society's

their the worker's decision of whether to get a vaccine ends up attracting whether other people get sick. The workers might not fully take all these other people's potential suffering into account when making her or his vaccination decision.

As Stanford University does many suggestions, understand this and tries to help them make the right decisions and so providers free flu vaccines for its staff and students.

Small pockets of unvaccinated individuals can allow a disease to gain a spread more widely well-being. For example, parent weighing the costs and benefits of a vaccine for their child is not always thinking of the consequences of that vaccination to other people. THese are markets in which subsidizing or regulating behavior can make everyone better off. Because the reason for requiring that a child be vaccinated before enrolling in school is not just to protect that child, because each child's vaccination affects others via potential contagions.

Robots take our jobs behavioral and economy influences

Robot job behavior brings economy influences

If one day robots can replace human to do simple, even complex jobs. They will bring what influences to our global societial economy.The popular economic refrain declares that the

global middle class is dying and robots will soon take our jobs, e.g. shopping center customer service jobs, library service jobs, cinema ticket sale jobs, restaurant kitchen cooker jobs,

even, bus drivers, taxi drivers etc. public transport driving jobs, accountant, doctors etc. professional jobs. Whether it is beautiful or petty matter if our future societies have many human jobs can be replaced to do from robots.

Businessman must may reduce to employ employees and reduce to pay salary or wage, when robots can be replaced to do their employees tasks. But, societies must bring unemployement rate rises , due to societies will have many people loss jobs when their employers choose to buy robots to serve their clients or do any office tasks or customer service or cleaning etc. tasks.

In micro economy view, employers may save money in long term, but in macro economy view, it will cause unemployment ratio rises , even crime rate rises when there are many people lose

jobs in societies. These models of doom, though, fail to account for the hundreds of businesses riding the waves of change in their industries when robots may be invented to replace human to do many simple , even complex tasks in our future societies.

WE may image that one small factory needs to manufacture fishes canes to sell to supermarket, the small , cheaper stuff and higher margin parts of the fishes manufacture industry. Before, this factory needs to employe many human factory workers need to help every fresh customer makeing the perfect fishing gear, designed for performance, durability, and cost in order to achieve to manufacture every fish cane in whole fished processing manufacturing stages. Every worker needs to spend about 15 to twenty minutes to finish every fish cane , till to delivery to any supermarket to sell. If this fish canes manufacturing factory can apply manufacturing robots to help them to finish any one working tasks , every robot can only spend five minutes to finish whole fresh fish cane manufacturing process. Thus, every robot can

help this factory save 10 to 15 minutes time to finsh every fish cane manufacturing process. IN fact, time is money, because when every robot can help this factory to reduce 10 to 15 minutes time to compare human worker. Then, this factory can finish about 20 fish canes in one hour if it can use robot to help it to manufacture fish canes. Otherwise, if this factory still use human workers to help it to manufacture fish canes, then it can finsh about 3 to 4 fish canes in one hour. SO, the manufacturing efficiency ensures that robots must help this fish manufacturing factory to raise fish canes number more than human workers. So, in robotic behavioral economy view, manufacturing robots must help this fish canes manufacturing factory to raise fish canes manufacturing number and deliver increasing number to supermarkets to prepare to sell every day. Robots can help this fish canes manufacturing factory bring manufacturing time saving,

rising manufacturing efficiency, improving performance and reducing wages expenditure long time advantages in micro economy view. However, manufacturing robots can also bring disadvanages to society, e.g. increasing unemployment ratio, increasing crime rate,
this factory workers will lose jobs and income, they need earn social welfare from government and increasing government finance pressure in short time, even long time in macro economic view.

Stanford University graduate program in economics, Scott lecturer explained that "in demand and supply economic theory for robots supply and demand case, robots supply number increasing may influence human workers demand number decrease. It sometimes calls " the efficient frontier".

No specific human beings were mentioned in any of economics classes. As robots supply and demand in market case, They (robots) may be purely theoretical " agents" who reached to the most reasonable sale prices in order to persuade any one businessman buyer to make manufacturing robot buying decision whether robots can help him / her to bring how much saving time , saving money, saving cost, improving performance, efficiency economic benefit before he/she plans to reduce workers number when he/ she decides to apply robots to replace human workers in his/her factory or office or any service department, e.g. cinema ticket sale service, shopping center customer service, shopping center cleaning , supermarket customer service etc. service or sale tasks. When robots can replace human to do any one of these tasks in any organizations. So, robots may be human worker agents who reached to prices the way robots would react to a software
command. There was nothing that explained why some people thrived and others did n't or why truly brilliant, hardworking people could fail when much lazier folks succeeded." Having been admitted to the Stanford University graduate program in economics, Scott lecturer hoped to get his answers there.

How robots influence our future social changing? Using the right technology can be a boon to your business in this economy. For internet example, it is easier than ever to find well-matched customers all around the world, to stay in contact with them, and to more quickly design the products they want. If you focus solely on being cutting -edge, though you risk letting the technology
take over what should be very robust relationships with your customers , employees, and colleagues. IN nowaddays society, technoligical advances

and cutomation, personal

relationships in business are more crucial than ever. I mean that robots can not replace human to serve clients to let them to feel more comfortable and passion more easily. For shoe shop case example, if the shoe shop apply one robot to serve its clients to replace human shoe salesperson to serve its shoe customers. Robots ensure that they can not persuade every shoe potential buyer to make shoe buying decision more easily when robots need to contact every shoe potential buyer. The reason is simple, because robots can not touch any one shoe buyer individual emotion very easier.

If the shoe buyer needs the robots to help him/her to choose any right shoe styles when he/she can not feel himself / herself can make the most right shoe style choice decision. The robots can not replace human shoe salesperson to make shoe style choice judgement more easily. They must need longer time to analyze whether which shoe style may be the most suitable to the shoe buyer. Otherwise, human shoe salesperson may attempt to make the most right shoe style choice decision to help any one shoe buyer to chooce the most right style shoe because he/she owns shoe style sale experience, shoe style knowledge, the most important reason is that they can feel every shoe customer individual emotion to touch whether he/she will feel comfortable or happy when they attempt to help every shoe customer to seek the most right shoe style in every shoe customer whole shoe searching processing. Othwerwise, serving robots are only one machine, they can not touch or feel every shoe customer individual emotion whether he/she feel comfortable or unhappy or happy when they need to contact them in whole shoe searching processing. Hence, I believe that some tasks robots can

not repalce human staff to do very easily. Otherwise, robots may bring disadvanatges to let any one businessman to loss his/her customers, due to robots can not touch every customer

emotion to compare human staff in service tasks more easily. Robots serving customer behaviors may cause money lose and customers number lose to the shop in micro economic view.

Intellectual human economic behaviors

What does intellectual human economic behaviors mean ? I believe that when we choose or decide to do intellectual behaviors, then our societies will be influenced to bring economic growth in consequence.I shall attempt to indicate pollution case to explain how and why eithet our intellectual or foolish behaviors may bring economic growth or recession in consequence as below:

On one hand, for air pollution social case aspect example, if we only consider to buy cars to drive for working aimr or holiday leisure aim. Then, our societies air will be polluted. Our health will be influenced to bad. Our car driving behaviors may cause global environment air pollution serously. In long tiem, global air pollution will bring our bodies health to be bad. Although, ourselves car driving behaviors may bring our driving travelling leisure enjoyment and comfortable feeling in short time, also we so not need to pay public transport fare often, but we need to compensate ourselves health economic intangible loss due to air pollution , when cars number increases, dirty air will cause ouselves health to become bad.

In the result, we will need to pay more medical expenditure when we are old age, due to ourselves bodies will become bad, due to we breathe global dirty air every day, due to ourselves cars pollute air in long time, e.g. 10 to 20 years, even 30 more without limited air pollution environment. So, driving cars behavior may be one kind of human foolish behavior and our foolish behavior may bring ourselves future long time medical expenditure absolutely.

One the other hand, water pollution social aspect, if we often keep much rubblish to pollute sea, oil exploration porcessing pollute ocean , ships gas pollute ocaen, then fishes will eat polluted food and drive dirty water, due to global ocean is polluted.

In fact, because human only to conside how to buy boats to carry on leisure enjoyment activities, or catch cruises to travel on the sea. Also, oil manufacturers only consider researching anywhere to find new oil exploration places to manufacture oil product, when their oil exploration processes pollute ocarn . Consequently, global fishes drink polluted warer or eat polluted food. They will have poison. SO, human will have high chance to eat poison polluted fishes, due to fishes are poison or are polluted.

So, human is doing foolish activities, we only hope to find oil exploration places to pollute ocean or we only spend money to buy ticket to catch ships to travel anywhere in global ocean. All of these human foolish behaviors will bring pollution to global ocean. On consequently, we will need to compensate to eat polluted or dirty or poision fishes, ourselves bodies health will be bad. In long time, we need have high chance to pay medical expenditure when we are old. So, pollution case may be one good example to explain how and why human foolish behavior may influence ourselves future need to compensate serious medical loss.

All of these human foolish behavior will bring pollution to global ocean. On consequently, we will need to compensate to eat polluted or dirty or poison fished , ourselves bodies health will be bad. In long time, we will have high chance to pay medical expenditure, when we are old. So, pollution case may be one good example to explain how and why human ourselves intellectual or foolish behaviors may influence future long time economic loss or economic growth or recession in micro and micro economic view.

On another water pollution aspect hand, if we often keep rubbish to sea, oil exploration processing pollutes ocean and ships' gas pollute ocean, then fishes will eat polluted food and drink dirty water, due to fishes will eat polluted food and drink dirty sea water because the global ocean is polluted seriously.

In fact, because human only consider how to buy boats to carry on any leisure water activities, or catches cruises to travel on the sea. Also, oil manufacturers only consider any where to find oil exploratin places to manufacture oil products from ocean, when their pol exploration processes can plooute ocean. Consequently, global fishes drink polluted water or eat direty food. They will have poison. So, human will have high chance to eat poison fishes.

Otherwise, such as pollutin case, it can infuence inflation or deflation. Consequently, the reason indicates supply and demand theory. If air pollution is serious, then we will consider health issue, global cars demand number may be influenced to reduce, when global cars number demand will reduce, global car prices and supply number will need to change to fall down in order to attract or persuade global car consumers choose to make car purchase decision.

Hence, global car manufacture number and car price will be influenced to reduce, due to global air pollution issue. Consequently, deflation will occur because when the country citizen usually does not spend much extra saving money to buy car expensive goods. Money value will be low. Otherwise, if global cair pollution is not serious, human considers to buy cars to enjoy driving leisure lives. So, global car demand is influenced to increase , also global car price will also influenced to increase.

Consequently, gobal human will choose to buy cars to drive. Due to we accept to spend extra saving to buy expensive car goods. Car sale price and supply may be influenced to rise up. Money value is influenced to reduce. Inflation may be influenced, due to global car consumers number increases, we would not have extra money to spend easily. Car expensive goods expenditure influences our spending habit to avoid to make car purchase decision more easily. So, human intellectual or foolish activities may bring inflation or deflation consequency in possible indirectly in macro economic view.

On conclusion, above pollution case explain that how and why human intellectual or foolish economic behaviors may bring inflation or deflation consequency as wll as economic growth or recession consequency as well as any goods demand and supply increasing or decreasing consequency. It implies that human behavior may have indirect relationship to influence any goods demand and supply number to either increase or decrease result as well as any goods price will be influenced to increase or decrease in micro and macro economic view.

The relationship between social change and human behavior

Why does economic changes may influence human individual behavioral change? I shall attempt to indicate shopping behavior and staying at home behavior to explain their case and effect relationsip as below:

Human behavior can be influenced by economic change or economic change can be influenced by human behavior? Why does recession may influence consumers reduce shopping desire? In social recession suitation, it is possible that many people lose jobs suddenly, due to businessmen lose many customers. They need to make decision to reduce employees number in order to continue to keep businesses. Consequently, many firms (organizations) their employees may lose jobs. When they have much time, due to lose jobs, they will feel to avoid to spend too much time and money to go to shopping often. Many losing jobs people, they will often stay at homes. So, they will reduce time to go to shopping, then non essential products won't their preferable choice purchase products. Hence, recession will change many losing jobs people their shopping or consumption desires to avoid to buy non essential products often . Usually when economic boom, many people have jobs to do because consumers number must increase when many people have jobs to do. Then, many people can accept to spend money to buy non essential products often. Many people feel spend time to go to shopping can satisfy their purchase of any kinds of new products useful psychology or desire. So, recession is one good example to explain it can influence many people do not like often to leave homes to go to shopping easily. Many people like to stay at homes, becaue they feel worry about spending too much shopping time when they leave homes. Their staying home time is one good negative shopping behavior example. So, economic change may influence human individual behavior changes , they have direct cause and efect relationship in behavioral economic view.

May human behavior influence economic change? Is it possible that human behavior may bring the country social economic change in macro economic or micro behavioral economic view ? I shall indicate publishing industry example. Do you feel that if there are many students feel learning is very important when they read many books or many of students feel interesting to read or they have reading new books in habit, then it is possible that the country will have many students like to spend time to go to any book shops to choose the books, they feel that they can help they learn new knowledge. Then the country will increase students number, they often spend time to visit any one book shop every week. Their visiting book shops behavior which may become their habits. So, the country will increase students number, they often spend time to visit book shops. Also, it implies that visiting book shops behaviors may be their behavioral habits.

So, when the country has many students often spend time to visit book shops , their visiting book shops behaviors may help any one book shop to raise books sale chance. So, the country's student individual often visiting book shop behaviors, their habitual visiting book shops behaviors must may assist help any one book shop to increase books sale number absolutely.

Consequently, any one book shop , its books sale bumber must be influenced to increase to increase because the country will have many students like or feel need visit book shops habit in order to choose any suitable books to buy to read at home in order to raise themselves learning effort. When the country has many bok shops often have many students visit their book shops, then their books sale number may be influenced to increase. It explain why student individual visiting book shop behavior may help any one book shop sale number increases also.

How human productive behavior may influence economic development

May any country which citizen behavior assist themselves country development? It is one cause and effect economic question. I mean that if the country itself citicen can not concentrate mind or energy to choose to do one kind of industry in order to let themselves country can bring the most benefit, then whether the counry itself economy can bring the most serious economic benefit. I shall attempt to indicate these countries themselves indistry choice to explain whether these countries themselves citizen productive behavior may help themselves countries to achieve the largest economic benefits. I shall indicate as below:

New Zealand farmer individual wine productive behavior

For New Zealand country example, this country concerns itself effort is foucs on farming agricultural aspect. So, this country has many farmers concentrate on farming agricultural aspect. May New Zealanders choose to spend time to produce different kinds of wines, e.g. wine or red grape wine is for the people are eating meat, or they are eating dinner.

When these New Zealanders their behaviors choose to do farming or agriculture to grow and produce different kinds of taste of white or red grape wine drinking products job. Themselves grape agriculture behavior will influence these New Zealanders themselves, they can learn how to improve different kinds of grape wine drinking products in order to achieve every kinds of white or read grape wines taste improving aim during their white or red grape producing process.

Why can New Zealander every individual white or read grape wine producers improve their white or read grape wine taste more easily? In behavioral economic view, it can explain that why any one New Zealander white or read grape wine producer can be encouraged or excited or persuaded to concentrate nervous and energy and effort to learn how to improve their white or red grape wine products easily.

In fact, New Zealand is one agricultural food export country. It has good natural environment resource , e.g. land, seed to provide any one farmer to produce themselves any kinds of agricultrual food products, e.g. fruit, or wine food products. Because New Zealanders know themselves country has enough natural resource . So, in common, many New Zealanders choose to attempt to do farming agricultural jobs in order to export themselves any kinds of fruit or meat or wine products to overseas or sell to domestic in order to earn profit.

So, when these New Zealand farmers number has been increasing every year. This country farmers will feel themsleves competition between this New Zealand farmers themselves are serious due to they may feel New Zealanders choose to do agriculture businesses in order to export themselves different kinds of farming food to overseas or sell to local to earn profit.

Hence, when many New Zealand farmers feel that farmers number has been increasing every year. They will feel themselves competition is serious. They must need to spend much time and nervous and effort to research what method is the best how to produce the best taste of white or red grape wine products in order to let local or overseas wine buyers to choose to buy his/her producing white or read grpae products to drink.

Hence, in competition psychological view, may influence many New Zealand white or reaad wine producers had been beginning to change their learning behavior on researching what method is the best in order to produce the best quality of taste red or white wine products to sell in order to attract overseas or local white or read grape wine drinkers to choose to buy his/her wine products. Their behavior will focus on learning how to raising or improving white or read grape wine taste method more than only focus on producing a large number white or red grape wine products. They believe wine quality is more important to compare wine producing number. So, New Zealand wine producers themselves wine producers behaviors have been changing on concentrating on researching wine quality method aspect more then wine producing number aspect in behavioral economic view.

America high technological productive behavior

For America example, US is one high technological country, it owns many high technological knowledge talent inventors, e.g. computer science inventors. Hence, US must attract many diferent countries owning high technological computer inventors choose to go to US to develop their computer science profession career. Also, it seems that when many computer science inventors or professions choose to go to US to develop themselves computer science new career. In behavioral economic view, due to their leaving themselves countries choice, which may bring influence themselve country job behaviors need to be changed. They must need to adapt US new live. Because they will forgive their past computer science job. These computer science professionals need to spend time to adapt US new lives. They " past computer science job behaviors" will need to be changed to their new US any computer employer's new computer science job model.

Because their traditional computer science jobs needed to be forgot in their themselves countries. They will feel their old computer science job knowledge and behavior needed to change in order to let their US any one new of computer company employer feels satisfactory to accept their new working behavior in any one US computer organization.

So, on the other hand, many US computer company employer will feel that they must need time to accept any one new overseas computer science professions their working behaviors, their working attitude daily, because these foreign comouter science professional, their past computer working behaviors and working attitude must be different to US domestic computer science professions.

In behavioral economic view, these overseas computer science professions, their working behaviors and attitude must be needed to change in order to adapt any one US new computer company itself domestic or local computer science professional stafs themselves daily working behaviors and attitude because these overseas and local computer science professionals must need to team work together.

In behavioral economic view, it is only one way that foreign computer science professionals must need to change themselves past country traditiona daily working behaviors and attitude in order to cooperate with these US local computer science professionals in teams more easily.

Consequently, if these foreign compute science professionals can change their past working behaviors and attitude to let any one US local computer science professional feels to cooperate with them easily in short time. Then, the US computer company itself whole computer professional teams themselves efficiencies will be influenced to raised or improved by the changing past working attitude and working behaviors of these foreign computer science professionals. So, in behavioral economic view, only if US any one computer company hopes itself computer teams themselves efficiency can be raised or improved when it decides to employ foreign computer science professionals and US domestic computer science professionals. They need to work in teams together. They must need to let these foreign computer science professionals to know how to change their working behaviors and attitude to let their domestic computer science professionals feel easy to work together. Then, the US computer company itself whole team efficiency must be rasied or improved easily in short time.

● China share market investing behavior

For China share market example, economic development depends on financial market. Because if many Chinese have interest to invest to carry on shares buying and selling activities in orde to learn how to earn shares interest and share profit when the China shareholder can make decision to sell himself/herself shares in the the high price, then he/she can earn money when he/she can sell the China company's shares in the high sale share price position.

If China has many Chinese like to spend time to carry on investing shares activities. Themselves shares buying and selling behaviors will influence

China has many companies can increase fund from many Chinese shareholders in order to have enough money to expand or develop themselves businesses in China in long term.

Consequently, when China can have many Chinese like to attempt to carry on buying and selling shares investing behaviors in China share market. Themselves buying and selling shares behaviors can help many Chinese companies have effort to increase enough money or capital in order to continue to do their businesses in long term absolutely. So, it explains why when many Chinese become shareholders , they can assist China will have many companies continue to develop their businesses if many Chinese like to carry on shares buying and selling investing behaviors in long time in China financial investment market nowadays in behavioral economic view.

Why has any individual country have many people invest share behavior which can influence the country's macro consumption desire?

I shall apply shares market buying and selling investment behavior to explaiin why shares investment behavior which may impact the country's overal consumption desire as below:

In behavioral economic view, I assume that when the coutry has many people have interest to attempt to carry on shares buying and selling investment behavior, then their frequent shares buying and selling behaviors which may bring negactive consumption desire or shopping desire of these shares investors their consumer behavior.

The reason is simple, when the country has many share buyers number suddenly been increasing rapidly. Consequently, these large group share investors must need to spend much time to research any kinds of company shares variations, whether when their share prices will rise up of fall down in order to achieve buying the company's shares in the lowest price and selling the company's shares in the highest price level in order to earn profit.

Basic on this reason, they must need to spend much extra time to research share prices changing behavior every day, e.g. one working person will wait to leave his/her job, after he/she can spend time to gather data to research the day's share price changing behavior after dinner. So, the working person's right time may be his/her share price market research behavior. Before he/she may spend his/her night time to go to shopping after dinner, but nowadays, he/she will fogive to do his/her shopping behavior before dinner or after dinner at hight sometime. He/she will make decision to spend much night time to turn on computer to click on share market website to research his/her share purchase choice to investigate whether his/her share price whether it rises up or falls down at the moment in order to make his/her share buying or selling decision at ever night time.

I mean the when the country has many people are share investors, their shares investment behavioral spenging time which will influence many shops lose customers at might often because the country will have many people feel need to spend night time to turn on computer or watch television to investigate share price variation. So, the country will have many people / share investors choose to stay at home in order to carry on share price variation investigation behavior, they need to listen share market update news from radios or watch the share market update news from computer or TV at home every night. Consequenly, they must reduce times to leave themselves homes at night. So, their shopping behavior also will be reduced. Because these share investors feel need to spend time to investigate share price variation news at homes which can bring economic benefits (high opportunity benefits) when they choose to forgive to leave homes to go to shopping times (opportunity cost) every night.

On conclusion, it seems that when the country has many people are share investors, then their share price investigating behavior may bring negative shopping emotion at night. Consequently, the country's any one shop may lose many customers from this share investor consumer group in behavioral economic view. Hence, when the country's share investors number had been increasing rapidly, it will influence any shops lose many customers from this share investing customer group at night frequenly in short time, even long time in behavioral economic view, because their shopping desires or shopping emotion will be brought negative feeling when they make decisions to spend much time to listen radios or watch TV or computers share price update nes at night. Hence, share market will bring negative impact to influence consumer shopping desire or negative shopping emotion in behavioral economic view.

Can technology influence human shopping behavioral change?
Nowadays, technological development has reached mature stage, whether technological mature stage may bring positive or negative shopping emotion influence to global consumers. I shall aplly internet inventin or ecommerce shopping channel tool to explain whether internet technology can bring postive or negative influence to global consumer behavior in behavioral economic view.

Internet is a good technological tool, it brings e-commerce business chance. In fact, commonly, global has have many businessmen choose to use internet channel to carry on their products transactions between global online-buyers and their electronic websites. So, global many shoppers had begun to feel online shopping is more convenient to compare visiting shops shopping. Their shopping behaviors have been changed from internet technological tool. Global has many shoppers choose to buy any products from any overseas or local businessmen their web stores. They only need to spend time to find any businessmen their webstores to choose the most suitable products to pay visa to buy from their webstores. at homes. So, in general, global had have may shoppers had changed their shopping behaviors from visiting shops to visiting webstores at homes often.

So, it seems that internet technological tool had influenced global many shops disappear, but internet webstores will be replaced their actual shops on streets. Some of businessmen either they choose webstores to replace shops or choose websotes and shops both or still keep shops only. Hence, internet tool influences global businessmen have three kinds of products sale channels to let globa local and overseas consumers to choose how to buy their products.

However, in fact, many of global shoppers, youngers and olders had begun to accept to buy any products from webstores. They feel to spend time to leave homes to visit shops , their shopping behaviors will be wasted time to not essential part to their daily lives. Hence, since internet technological invention, it had changed many consumers their traditional visiting shops shopping habit to change to buying products from webstores channel.

However, on the one hand, internet creates webstores ecommerce shopping channel to let global many consumers do not need to leave homes to go to shopping. It brings negative visiting shops shopping emotion to global general consumers nowadays. But on the other hand, it also brings positive visiting internet webstores shopping emotion to global general consumer nowadays. So, it seems that global many consumers feel that they often do not need to spend much time to go out shopping. Many global consumers feel convenient and enjoy to choose any products to buy from different internet webstores, when the online buyer chooses the most suitable product, he she only needs to pay visa card to buy the product from the online seller's webstore conveniently at home.

Hence, online shopping can bring economic benefit to online buyers, e.g. avoiding walking time or spending transport fare to visit the shop to go to shopping, shortening or reducing shopping time to do another important matter.

On conclusion, global many consumers began feel online shopping can bring more economic benefits on shortening shopping time, avoiding transport fare spending aspect. So, online shopping will be popular shopping behavior for future long time. It may encourage global many shoppers can make rapid shopping decision in short time in order to carry on any products buying transaction to global any one online shopper in short time easily in behavioral economic view. So, global many businessmen had begun to build themselves one attraction webstore in order to persuade different countries consumers to choose to click themselves webstores from internet channel to buy any kinds of products in short time easily.

So, internet technology had changed consumers traditional shopping behaviors to build positive online shopping emotion as well as raise online sellers' any products sale chance easily in behavioral economic view.

Why and how human behavior may influence the country's economic growth or recession?

When one country has many people choose to do the same matter for one period, whether their behavior may influence the country's pvera; economic growth or recession . I shall attempt to indicate cases toexplain their relationship as below:

For flowing rubblish behavioral case example, do you feel that when the country has many people often flow rubblish on the streets, instead of their flowing rubblish behavior may bring streets dirty? But, their flowing rubblish behavior may explain that this country has people may have enough money to buy food to ear, or enough cloths to wear, enough bottles of water to drink, even they may have enough money to buy new television, radio, refrigeraters , washing machines, desktops or laptops electronic home products from old to new to use in order to satisfy their living needs. So, when they flow old electronic home products, their flowing old home electronic products behaviors may seem that they have enough money to buy other new home electronic products to replace old home electronic products to use at homes.

However, it seems thaat this country ought have many people have jobs to do. So, many of them, they can easy to make purchase decison to flow any old home electronic products and buy any new home electronic products to use . Because this country has many people have jobs to do. So, they can often not use old home electonic products to become rubblishs to flow on streets after they had bought any kinds of new home electronic homes.

In fact, it also implies that this country's economy grows rapidly. So, many businesses can glow up rapdly. When they expanded their businesses, they must need to increase employees number in order to let they help themselves to raise productivity or serve their clients absolutely. So, when the country has many businesses can grow up, it seems that its economy must be better or it is improved to compare past. Due to many different kinds of home electronic products had been often bought to use by this country people in this period. So, this country's any streets can be observed that expensive electronic home products were flowed on streets anywhere. then, this country will have many electronic home products sellers can sell their home electronic products very easily. When this country has many people can find any kinds of jobs to do easily. So, due to unemploymen rate had been decreasing.

In behavioral economic view, as this many electronic home products rubblish country case, we can observe this country may have many people have jobs to do. So, consumption number has been increased long time. So, cheap food, or expensive home electronic products may be rubblish on any streets. This country's people , their flowing rubblish behaviors may be explained that many of people have enough jobs to do, so they have ability to buy any good taste food to eat or buy any kinds of expensive electronic home products to use. So, this country's economy may be improved for this long period. So, in behavioral economic view, when this country can have many electronic home products rubblishs are flowed on anywherer in streets frequently. It seems that this country will have many people have jobs to do, so it causes they often change old home electronic products or replaced them easily, when they have enough income to spend to buy any kinds of new home electronic products to use at homes easily. Moreover, their flowing old electronic home products behaviors also indicate that this country has many people their salaries may be increased in possible from their emplyers. When this country can have many different kinds of home electornic products are sold. It means that this country's electronic home products needs or demand had been increasing, due to many people have jobs to do and income increases to excite their living of needs also improve. Consequently, this country may seem have better economic improvement. We can observe from this country's electronic home products rubblish increasing income in theis period.

On conclusion, this country ought experience economic growth at this period. So, " flowing expensive electronic home rubblish increasing number " may seem that this country's economic growth is rapidly in this period, due to many people have jobs to do as well as salaries increase in this period.

Technology how impacts human behavior changing?
Technology how influences human behavior to bring changing? For example, online share purchase and sale transaction from smart phone brings share investor can do share buying or selling transation in any where and any time conveniently, non manual driving auto vehicle, bring car owner feels comfortable and spends free time to do other matter, e.g. reading, listening mucis in himself or herself car freely. electrical energy vehicle can help car owner to reduce air polluton and it can brings the drivers do not feel drive long time in any journeys in order to avoid air pollution for environmental protection responsible car drivers in our societies. Thus, they will drive long time in any journeys when they can drive electronic energy cars to replace oil energy cars.

However, online technology can also bring consumers can choose to stay at homes to buy any things from seller individual online webstore conveniently. Such as online technology can bring shoppers do not need to spend much time to visit shops to buy any things. They can choose any kinds of products from any online sellers individual online webstores conveniently at homes. Online technology excite busy consumers can make purchase decision easily as well as it can help online sellers sell any kinds of products from internet easily.

In behavioral economic view, technology can change human behavior to be improved, it can let human feels comfortable, more free time ro use, rapid making any decisions, such as apply smart phones to make share purchase or sale transaction decision, online shopping decision, even travelling any where decision in short time, when the traveller finds the most cheap hotel accommodation room price and air ticket price frm any travel agent online tourism webstore, then the potential travel customer can follow the online hotel accommodation price and air ticket price data to make decision when to buy the air ticket from the airline travel agent or make decision when to prebook which hotel accommodation room to go to the country to travel from online travel agent tourism webstores. So, technology can encourage global any country travelers to make anywhere to trvel rapidly. If the traveler can find the country's general hotel rooms and airline tickets prices had been decreasing more sightly. The traveler may make travel decision to choose the country to travel in short time, then he/she can prebook the country;s any hotel room and airline ticket to pay by visa fraom the country's any hotel and airline travel agent webstores., before one week, even one month or more easily. Hence, online technology can also encourage traveler individual frequent travel times to be increased, due to global travelers can find any hotel rooms and airline tickets prices from internet conveniently at homes. They do not need to spend time to visit any airline travel agent to enquire travel choice country's hotel rooms prices and airline ticket prices. They can compare global travel of countries choices ' all hotels rooms and airline agents air tickets prices to make prebook airline seat and hotel room decision before one week, one month even six months early.

On conclusion, online technology can encourage global travelers can make travelling any where and when traveling time desicions easily. It can excite tourism industry develops in long time. Also, such as electricity cars invention can encourage environment protection car owners do car purchase decision easily, because they can choose to drive electronic energy cars to replace oil energy cars in order to avoid air pollution occurs easily. So, electronic cars can increase electronic car purchasrs number, due to many of environmental protection attitude of car owners can choose to drive electricity cars to bring air cleans, even non -manual driving cars can encourage lazy driving and free time driving car owners to choose to buy non-manual (artificial intelligent) cars to drive , because they can spend much free time to read, listen music or do any matters in themselves cars, they do not need to drive cars, robotic (AI) auto driving machine is such one non-manual driver to help them to drive themselves cars confidently. So, non-manual driving cars can attract lazy and enjoying free time driving car owners to choose to buy to replace traditional manual cars to drive easily. Moreover, online share transaction can help any share investors to make share buying and selling decision in short time easily. When they can apply smart phones technological tool to carry on share buying and selling activities easily. They can observe any share rising or falling price suitation from smart phones in any where any any time easily. So, smart phone technology can help global any shareholders to make share purchase and sale transaction easily. So, technology can encourage human makes decision in short time rapidly.

How and why employees behaviors may influence economy development?

In behavioral economy view,I believe the country's any organizational employees behavior may bring indirect relationship to influence the country's long term economic development. I shall indicate past manufacture industry social development period to explain their relationship. For many countries' past business activities had belonged to manufacturing industry, such as US, UK past before 1980 year, it focused on steel manufacturing and steel manufacturing related machine products. So, US, Uk developed countries manufacturing industries may be past main country's economic income sources. I assume US , UK past had one million number different kinds of industries. They ought had about seven houndred thousand number organizational businesses were belonged to manufactured industry. They may include:

Steel manufacturing and steel related machine manufacturing, e.g. vehicle manufacturing, home appliances, e.g. washing machine, television, radio, refrigerate cooler, heater, air condition etc. different kinds of different kinds of steel -related manufacturing machine, they were manufactured from US, UK steel machine manufacturers. So, US, Uk the other three hundred thousand number industry may be general service industry, e.g. hotel service, restaurent, cinema, public transport service, tourism lesiure , wine bar, supermarket etc. different kinds of non-manufacturing industries business organizations were operated in UK, US past before 1980 year.

So, in UK, US developed countries industry development history, they ought have high percentage of businesses belonged to steel related manufacturing machine and steel products. Also, in the past before 1980 year, US, Uk business employers , they employed many workers are manufacturing workers. They needed to spend long time to work in factories. They were skillful workers, and they are trained to manufacturing cars, washing machine, television, heater, etc. even steel itself different kinds of steel related products to prepare to deliver to their shops to sell to US, Uk local or overseas clients.

So, I believe that past UK, US ought employ many employees, they belonged to skillful manufacturing workers, manufacture increasing steel machine or steel related machine number of products rapidly daily. So, if UK, US had had many of these manufacturing factories owned high skillful workers, then their manufacturing steel-related machine or steel both kinds of products number must be influenced to raise rapidly. Consequently, their steel machine manufacturing products would been exported to overseas or would been sold to local both markets , they may be influenced to raise sale number. They (these manufacturing workers) needed to be trained to know how to manufactur these different kinds of machine products in the efficient teams and they ought to be trained to raise their efficiencies in order to shorten time to manufacturing many kinds of steel related manufacturing machine or steel itself products rapidly. So , if their efficiencies and manufacturing performance was improved, these US, UK any one manufacturing worker and their teams ought achieve raising productivities significantly.

Hence, when past UK, US manufacturing industry development period, if these two countries' any manufacturing factories could have many manufacturing workers could be trained to be skillful and proficient manufacturing workers. Then, in past every day to these factories workers, they ought help their steel or steel related manufacturing employers to raise any kinds of machine or steel products number in every team. So, when past in the manufacturing industry development, US, UK could have many factories' manufacturing workers themselves steel or steel related machine products manufacturing skill could be trained to to improve to any kinds of these machine or steel manufacuring products quality as well as their products number could be influenced to raise by themselves skillful improvement significantly every day.

Then, what would be influenced to occur to past UK, US manufacturing industry period? In behavioral economic view, when these two manufacturing industry developed countries, such as UK, US , if they had many factories workers can be trained to improve their skill in order to achieve any kinds of steel or steel-related machine products quality could be improved as well as products manufacturing number could be also increased absolutely.

In consequence, past UK and US both countries ought increase themselves any kinds of steel and steel related machine products number to be supplied to themselves local shops to let local clients to choose any one kind of machine manufacturing products to buy easily as well as they could also export to supply overseas any countries to buy their different kinds of steel or steel related machine products to let overseas steel or steel related manufacturing machine product buyers, they can have many of these different kinds of these steel or steel-related different kinds of manufacturing machine from UK and UK these both countries easily to compare other countries.

On conclusion, I believe that past US, and UK macro manufacturing industry income GDP would increase significantly. So, they would have good economic growth performance because when many of these manufacturing workers themselves manufacturing effort could be improved. So, it explained when employees manufacturing abilities can influence economic growth indirectly.

Robots invention whether they can help organizations to raise efficiencies or inefficiencies?

In behavioral economic view, in any organizations, when the organization hopes its worker teams can raise efficiencies , the organization may choose to increase more workers number and/or it can provide training to improve these workets themselves skills in order to raise their efficiencies. For one warehouse example, when the warehouse increases many goods , they are needed to delivered these goods from the shelves to the delivering destination locations. If this warehouse supervisors feel these workers themselves goods delivery speeds are slow, which is possible due to this warehouse's workers number is not enough. So, this warehouse supervisor ought increase workers number in order to increase their goods delivery speed in order to deliver goods from the shelves to every indicated goods delivery destination in order to let any one lorry driver can transport the right kinds of goods and ensure the accurate goods number to transport to any one client home rapidly.

However, if this warehouse supervisor planed to buy several warehouse goods delivery robots to assist these warehouse workers to find the right kinds of goods from shelves and then deliver to the right destination location in the warehouse. So, these warehouse orkers can concentrate on counting the accurate goods number and ensuring the right kinds of goods in order to prepare to let lorry drivers to transport these goods to these goods of buyers themselvers homes rapidly. Consequently, in the first step, robots can concentrate on finding th right goods from shelves and delivers them to the right goods transportation of location destination. Then, in the second step, these warehouse workers can concentrate on counting the accurate goods number and ensuring the right kinds of goods in order to prepare to put them to the lorry. Consequently, when warehouse robots and warehouse workers can cooperate to work together, the most important, robots, can deal on finding the right kinds of goods and deal on delivering the accurate number of goods of job duty as well as these warehouse workers can only concentrte on counting the right kinds of goods number in order to avoid it has none any mistake of wrong kinds of goods and inaccurate goods of delivery number to be transported to the lorry and to deliver to any one buyer's home.

So, it seems that warehouse robots ought help any one warehouse worker to raise himself efficiency and avoid goods delivery of mistake occurrence easily as well as their help to warehouse workers that can let any one goods buyer feels their goods can be delivered to their homes rapidly. Moreover, warehouse robots can also help these warehouse workers to raise efficiencies because warehouse robots can help them to shorten goods delivery time between any one shelf and any one goods delivery destination of location in the warehuse because robots may help them to find the right kinds of goods from the right shelf in the short time. So, any one worker does not need to spend long time to seek anywhere is the right shelf location for the kind of goods when the kind of goods are needed to deliver to the buyer's home from lorry. Warehouse robots can help them to do this aspect of " finding the goods from the right shelf in short time job duty". So, any one warehouse worker only needed tospend less time to do the counting of any right kind of goods number and ensuring the right kind of goods job duty. Consequently, this warehouse 's any one worker, his any one kind of goods delivery time may be reduced, because robots' assistance and they may have more confidence to avoid mistake to deliver the wrong number of goods and/or the wrong kind of goods to any one goods buyer's home.

On conclusion, it seems that warehouse robots ought may help any one warehouse worker to raise efficiency for any one team in the warehouse as well as the warehouse any one supervisor does not need to spend much time to observe any one worker individual performance for " goods delivery job duty aspect" because their goods delivery job duty that had been replaced to do by these several warehouse robots. Robots can achieve the more accurate of right kinds of goods and the right number of goods delviery job performance to compare any one of human warehouse worker themselves right kinds of goods of delivery and right number of goods of delivery job performance. So, when robots can participate to cooperate with this warehouse's any one worker to do their goods of delivery job duty in this warehouse every day. Then, robots can raies any one of supervisor individual confidence in order to let they do not need to spend time to observe any one of worker individual whose goods of delivery job performane. They can concentrate on supervising any one worker whose goods transport to lorry in the final step in order to avoid to deliver wrong goods number and / or wrong kind of goods to any one goods buyer's home every day. Consequently, this warehouse's overall teams of their delviery of goods performance many be improved by robotss' participatin to goods of delivery task as well as this warehouse's oveall teams themselves efficiencies may be influenced to raise by robots' goods of delivery task participation.

Why social behavior may influence organizational strategy needs to be changed ?

Why any organizations need to know whether nowadays social behaivor how has been changing in order to implement the kind of the most right strategy to achieve the profit aim pursue in possible. I shall indicate nowadays ecommerce or online, customer shopping behavior to explain above question concerns they ought have close relationship between social behavior and organizational strategic choice or organizational behavioral changing need.

On nowadays ecommerce business, or online shopping model, this kind of shopping model in global many young and old age consumers like to apply internet tool to choose any country sellers website stores in order to stay at home to buy any kinds of products from themselves webstores in global societies.

In fact, online shopping model had been popular for long time above to twenty years. Most of global sellers will make decision to design themselves webstores in order to attract global many online buyers to choose to buy their products from themselves webstores. So, it seems that social consumers purchase behaviors had been changed to online shopping from internet invention.

Hence, social consumers purchase behavioral changes may influence any organizations' strategies need to be changed from visiting shops purchase strategy model to online purchase strategy model, if the seller still concentrate on concentrate on considerate how to design itelf , but neglects to considerate how to design itself webstore, e.g. how to design attract product photos to put on itself webstore, how to arrange sale price information location to be putted on webstore and visa card payment location on itself webstore in order to let any one online buyer can feel very easier to buy itself any kinds of products from itself webstore. Then, its potential online buyers will be influenced to increase number when they can find this online seller itself any kinds of products photes and every kinds of product sale price information and visa card payment channel locations easily from itself webstore.

So, it implies that nowadays any one seller ought need to design one webstore to let any one online overseas and domestic consumers can have chance to click itself webstore to choose any one kind of product to buy conveniently when he/she does not hope to leave him/her home to go to shop, because nowadays social shopping behaviors had been influenced to change when internet invention, them it gives another online purchase method to replace visiting shops purchase method to global any one buyer in nowadays societies.

So, if nowadays any one seller still concentrate on how to design itself shop display in order to put any kinds of product on shelf in order to let any one visiting shop customer to find the kind of product to buy, but it neglects to change to choose to pursue another new technological shopping method, such as webstore purchase method in order to implement effective strategy to design the most right webstore as well as in order to attract global overseas and local consumers to find itself webstore easily from website and find its any one kind of product phots and sale price and visa card payment button in order to choose to buy itself any kinds of products in the short time. Consequently I believe that the seller will lose many customers from overseas and local when its other same or similar product sellers choose to design themselves webstores in order to let global any one product buyer can buy themselves any one kind of product when they can pay visa card to buy their products from them webstores conveniently when they stay at home habitly. Then, the seller will lose many global potential customers in long time.

On conclusion, in behavioral economic view, any consumer behavioral social changing, which will influence any in order to avoid customers number loses significantly . In future time, organizations need to make rapid decision in order to implement the most reasonable and the most useful strategy in order to avoid global potential customers number reduces or lose them in long time. So, social behavioral changing environment ought influence any global organizations need to decide how to change themselves strategies in order to avoid customers loses significantly in future time.

How and why human behavior may influence economic growth or recession?

May ourselves daily behaviors influence our global societial continue economic growth or recession? Do they have cause and effect close relationship between human behaviors and global economic growth or recession? I shall apply behavioral economic theory to analyze and explain whether ourselves daily behaviors and our global societial economic growth or recession which have close cause and effect relationship as below:

Every country itself economic development must depend on any business activities, otherwise, any kinds of business activities must need ourselves business activities or behaviors in order to achieve any business activities as well as achieve the country's overall economic development in macro view. However, any country's overall business activites or behaviors which must depend on any kinds of individual businessmen, themselves employees daily working behavior or activity or performance in order to help them to attract or increase many clients number to acieve " earning profit" aim. So, it seems that any individual business, itself overall every department individual working behavior is one main factor to influence the company's overall business performance.

For agricultural fruit and meat food farming industry example, such as New Zealand is a farming main target industry country. It had had many New Zealanders were daily themselves own farming businesses for many years. Their farming businesses include growing fruit, sheep, cow, pig pork, meat etc. food sale business. If the New Zealand farmer owned a large size farming land, then he will choose either growing fruit or feeding sheeps, pigs, cows to be meat to to transport to New Zealand supermarkets to help them to sell to their farmers meet to New Zealanders in order to earn profit. Thus, if the New Zealand farmer owned large size of farming lands, then he needs to employ many farming employees (farming workers) to help him to carry on farming business daily tasks, e.g. picking up friuts, feeding pigs, cows, sheeps to eat food daily. These daily farming jobs are very important to influence this New Zealand farmer's meats or fruits sale number whether they can be easy or diffcult to sell in New Zealand supermarkets , if these farming workers can own encough farming knowledge or skill to know how to pick up fruits method and make judgement to know whether it is right time to pick up the kind of fruits from the trees , as well as know how feed this pigs, sheeps, cows to eat food in order to let they are better health. Consequently, their farming behaviors which can let these animals can provide the best taste and enough meat from these animals to let New Zealander to buy to eat from New Zealand any one supermarket. Even these New Zealand farming workers can know whether the kinds of fruits, e.g. oranges, apples, gapes etc. fruits whether they ought be picked up from the trees at the right time. Consequently, they can make judgement to decide to pick up any kinds of the best taste fruits to let any one New Zealander to buy to eat from any one supermarket in New Zealand. Otherwise, if they do not make judegement to know whether the kind of fruit ought not be picked up because they still need longer time to continue grow up to increase fruit size and better taste from the trees in order to let any one fruit buyer can feel better taste when they eat this kind of fruit later. If they can buy this kind of fruit to eat later, then this New Zealand farmer's his fruit buyers can buy the best taste of this kind of fruit to eat from an yone supermarket in New Zealand. Consequently, many New Zealand supermarkets will choose to buy any kinds of fruits from this farmer fruit supplier when they feel this farmer's fruits can provide more better taste fruits to compare other farmers' fruits.

Thus, due to New Zealand is one farming main income source country. It's any kinds of fruits and meats need to be export to overseas to sell , instead of local sale. It's GDP percent is very high to whole country 's overall income source. So, any one New Zealand farmer individual and any one farming worker individual working behavior will influence its economy whether it is influenced to grow or recession possible. Moreover, it also seems that farming workers' farming knowledge and skill will influence themselves farming daily activities to achieve the aim of the number of increase or decrease to any kinds of fruits whether they are better taste or the number of increase of decrease to any kinds of meats whether they are better taste to supply to any one New Zealand fruit or meat buyers to eat from any one New Zealand supermarket. So, it implies that any one New Zealand farming worker individual farming behavior may influence any kinds of fruits or any kinds of meat taste because they are transported to any one supermarket to sell in New Zealand.

Consequently, if New Zealans had many farmers can teach god farming knowledge and skill to let their any one farming workers know how to decide judgement to decide when it is right time to pick up any kinds of fruits from trees , or how to grow them on soil in order to let they can grow rapidly. Then, many different kinds of fruits can be provided to let any one New Zealanders can eat the best taste of fruits when their fruits are supplied to any one New Zealand supermarkets. Even, if they knew how to feed foods to pigs, cows, sheeps to eat daily. Then they can be more health and they can provide the best taste of meats to let any one New Zealanders can buy their meats from any one New Zealand supermarkets. Moreover, their fruits and meats can be transported to overseas to let any one country fruits or meats buyers can choose any kinds of New Zealand meats and fruits to buy to eat from themselves countries supermarkets. Then, many overseas fruit and meat buyers will perfer to choose New Zealand any kinds of fruits or meats to buy to compare other countries fruits or meats to buy when they go to any one local supermarkets.

On conclusion, it seems that New Zealand farming workers themselves farming behavior may influence their farming employers any kinds of fruits or meats sale number and income because their farming task behaviors must influence whether their fruits or meats taste are the better taste or worse taste to compare their other local farmers (the farmer competitors) whose fruits or meats taste. If tthe farmer's any one farming worker can be trained to learn how to know to feed animals skill and when is the most right time to pick up any kinds of fruits from trees or how to grow them on the soil methods. Due to these farming worker individual farming behavior may influence his different finds of fruits and meats sale number to be increase or decrease, so these any one New Zealand farmer must need to depend on any one farming worker whose farming working methods, if their farming working behaviors can be the best to influence any kinds of fruits to grow rapid or any kinds of pigs, cows, sheeps animals grow up rapidly , then their sale number may be increase significantly and their taste can be improved to let any New Zealand or overseas meat or fruit buyer to buy to eat to feel from any one New Zealand or overseas supermarkets, then New Zealand's agriculture industry must be influenced to increase. In the world, any one fruit or meat buyer must choose to buy New Zealand's fruit and meat to eat in prefer to compare other countries' fruits and meats. So, New Zealand's GDP may be influenced to raise from any one New Zealand farming worker individual farming working behaviors.

Reasons why human behavior may influence economic recession or growth?

Can ourselves daily behaviors or activies influence ourselves countries' economic growth or recession? I shall attempt to explain the reasons why they have direct or indirect relationship between human behavior and economy growth or recession as below:

I shall indicate environment pollution case to attempt to explain above question. Our societies had been experiencing servious environment pollution challenge. However, environment pollution , such as air pollution is caused by air planes and vehicles emission by air planes and vehicles emission as well as water pollution is caused by plastic rubblish, or dirty water or oil or gas chemical material, these both kinds of pollution ought may bring economic recession and this both kinds of pollution are caused by human ourselves daily foolish activities.

I believe human behavior and economy and pollution which have cause and effect relationship. I shall analyze this environment pollution case to explain why they have case and effect relationship between human foolish behavior and environment pollution and economic recession as below:

When global societies had many people like to buy cars to drive to bring emission to fresh air on the roads as well as many manufacturing factories will bring emission to pollute fresh air in their manufacturing processes. Factories and cars will bring air pollution , due to factories need to pollute fresh air in order to manufacture many products and car owners need to drive their cars to go to offices or leisure places. Their cars will also bring emisson to pollute fresh air. On consequence, car owners themselves frequent driving behaviors and factory workers themselves frequent manufacturing behaviors may bring environment pollution. Technology or human behavior whether may influence economic growth or recession. Moreover, air planes also brings emission to pollute air when they are flying in sky. Also, when ships bring oil pollution or sea plastic rubblishs bring pollution to global oceans.

In fact, manufactuers and cars owners, such as factories workers manufacturing behaviours ans car owners driving behaviors and pilots driving air planes flying behaviors and ships transport behaviors, which may cause plastic rubblish, oil or gas emission to sky or sea or on the road to cause ocean and air pollution is serious. However, human ourselves need to buy cars to drive to satisfy ourselves driving leisure or enjoyment, travelers need to catch air planes to travel to enjoy leisure needs, factories workers need help factories to manufacture many products to sell to customers to satisfy their using needs. oil exploration needs to find lands to explore new oil lands.

All of these business and leisure activites may bring serious air and water pollution. However, due to serious air and water pollution will bring earth warming challenge , such as some countries temperature will be influences to rise up to 40 degree or higher br earth warming. However, earth warming is caused by air and ocean pollution. Pollution must be caused by human ourselves, driving cars leisure and factories manufacturing business activities. Hence, if human decided to continue to do these foolish behaviors, we only pursue to manufacture different kinds of industrial products or drive cars to enjoy leisure aims, but we also neglect ourselves behaviors may bring environment pollution. Then, earth warming or earth temperature will be influenced to rise up absolutely in long term. Moreover, if our future earth will be influenced to bring serious high temperature effect by human ourselves these foolish behaviors.

On consequencey, warth warming will bring serious economic losses in possible because when ourselves earth temperature had been influenced to rise up to 40 degree or high. Ourselves health will be caused poor, due to we will feel difficult breath, we must need often tried and hard to work, due to our nervous and health will be influenced to poor by pollution and earth warming effect. Also, we need to pay more money to see doctors when we had long life. Then, our societies will lose may strong labors to help manufacturers to work, e.g. factories will reduce workers number to help manufacturers to produce more different kinds of products, due to workers health is general poor. Due to lacking enough workers to manufacture products, our societies will begin to reduce enough supply number of products to sell to global consumers to satisfy their use needs.

On conclusion, in behaviroal economic view, our societies will lose many labors due to their bodies are not health by air and water pollution. Global economic and business activities will be influenced to worse by global workers reducing number reason. So, economic recession will begin to occur in possible when pollution reaches the serious level.

How employee behavior influences organizational development?

Can any organizational department employee individual behavior may help the organization to bring long term development? When one employee individual behavior, manager won't feel whose task behavior may help organizational development, but when the department has many teams cooperate to work together , all of these team employees whose task behaviors may help their organization to bring long term development.

I shall explain how any why when the organization has many departments, as well as when every team memmber individual behavior may help whole organization to bring long term development in possible as below:

Every organization must need efficient department to cooperate to work together. They may include human resource, finance, logistic, facility management, sales, marketing , operateional , warehouse , factory manufacture , research and development, purchase, customer service etc. different kinds of departments to cooperate to work together. So, any one employee individual behavior, include manager, leader, supervisor, worker, salesperson, manufacture worker, adminisration staff, factory or logistic worker etc. themselves task behavior whether his/her performance is worse or better , whose task behavior ought bring long term good or bad influence to cause the organization's whose efficiency, or performance , whether it can be influenced to improve significantly. For car factory manufacture workers department example, it exmploys 100 car manufacturing workers. They need to manufacture at least 50 cars in order to bring enough car manufacture number to supply to global car buyers to choose to buy (satisfaction to car buyers their driving leisure activity needs). However, if this car manufacture firm employs many low skilful car manufacture workers, their inefficient car skill may bring cars manufacture number reduces, they can not achieve to reach the at least 50 cars manufacture number, if these 100 car manufacture workers. They have half number of workers, they only manufacture 30 to 40 cars number at least daily. So, it seems that this car manufacture firm will have half car manufacture workers bring the low cars manufacture number to compare the another half cars manufacture workers, when this proficient car manufacture workers may manufacture at least 60 or more cars manufacture number daily. So, it explains that this inefficient car manufacture workers will not help this car manufacture company to manufacture enough cars number in order to supply to global car market to sell to satisfy global car buyers needs, when car buyers demand number is more thn car manufacture supply number in supply and demand view. Hence, in long term, if this car manufacture company can not employ new proficient car manufacture workers to replace those inefficient or low skillful car workers. Consequently, its car manufacture number must be influenced to reduce and it can not satisfy global car buyers driving leisure needs.

However, if this car manufacture firm also has shop to sell itself any kinds of cars, instead of manufacturing cars product. So, it needs have both main departments to help it to earn profit. The first step, it needs have proficient car manufacture workers to help it to manufacture at least 50 cars from every car worker in order to have enough cars number to be provided to global car sellers to help it to sell to global car customers. Second step, if it decided to attempt to sell itself cars. Then, it needs to set up car shops in global to different countries in order to let global car buyers may visit its global any one car shop to enquire any one car etc. salesperson about any car quality, speed, gas useful, price, safety, etc. information questions and they can attempt to sit in any one car to feel whether which car can let them to feel more comfortable to make final car purchase decision in any one shop. So, if this car company can provide good sale speaking skillful training to any one car salesperson to let his/her to know whether how to explain every kind of car function and feature, manufacture method etc. questions, then I believe that they can influence any one car buyer to makecar purchase choice decision more easily. So, it this car manufacturer hopes it may attempt to earn profit from different countries car sellers and car buyers both. It ought also provide training course to all general car salespeople to be proficient owning sale speaking skillful professional skill in order to prepare having more confidence to persuade any one car customer to make car purchase choice from any one car salesperson more easily to compare global other car sellers.

Hence, if this car manufacturer could build both car manufacturing team and car sale team more proficient. However, if this car manufacturer hopes to develop itself car manufacture busness to expend to car sale business both in success. It must need to spend long term to provide training courses to general car manufacture workers and general car salespeople both to be proficient car skillful manufacture workers and proficient car skillful salespeople in order to help they can manufacture enough car numbers and help they can persuade may car customers can make car purchase decision in short time when they visit its any one car shop.

However, this car manufacture company explains why every car manufacture worker whose manufacturing behavior and every car salesperson sale persuading speaking ability may help this car manufacture company to expand from its car manufacture market to car sale market development in sussess in possible. So, this car manufacture firm must need these two kinds of essential human resource elements in order to achieve its cars sale number and cars manufacture number increasing aim. They may include proficient car manufacture workers and proficient car salespeople both human resource elements. These both human resource daily task behavior may influence its long term task efficient performance in order to expand itself car sale business in success from itself car manufacture business easily. If it hopes to expand its car manufacture business to car sale business in success. It must need to provide training to these two departments general staffs to be proficient staffs in order to supply enough cars number to its global car shops to let global car buyers can choose its any kinds of cars to buy in any time.

Morevoer, if this car manufacture company can have good skillful of car research and development department , it aims to research and innovate any new technological cars invention in order to improve its any traditional old kinds of cars to be innovative new kinds of cars from every year. Consequently, its any new innovative cars ought attract global any one car buyer to make car purchase choice final decision more easily, because its any kinds of manufacturng cars can be innovated rapidly to compare its any one car manufacturing competitors, when its nay kinds of cars can be shorten time to innovate within three months, but its any one car manufacturing competitors need to spend more than three months, even one year to innovate themselves traditional old cars products in long term. Hence, its car staffs research and development department staffs must need own good car product design ability, proficient car engineering knowledge , even car invention knowledge in order to innovate its any one kind of car product in short time and introduce to let its global car proficient car buyers feel surprise to its any one kind of innovative car products to compare its any one car manufacturer.Hence, these four departments: car manufacture, car sale and car research and development anr car training departments must need concentrate resource to provide enough training to any one staffs in order to achieve the best performance.

On conclusion, all these departments staffs their performance can influence car manufacture aim to chance to car manufacture and sale aim more significantly. it explains why some main department staffs whole behaviors may influence any organizational performance significantly.

Artificial intelligent Human clever and art creating ability methods

How robots create human clever and art creating ability? Nowadays robots invention may help businesses to reduce employees number, improve performance, raise productivities, reduce cost in service industry,manufacturing industry, office , warehouse, restaurant, hotel , factory, cinema etc. different kinds of business environments, even public transport tools. However, instead of robots may bring these above advantages to any kinds of business working and service environments, whether robots may also help human to create clever and image creating ability. I shall attempt to answer this question:

On the one hand, I believe that past technology ,e.g. machine , it should not have ability to help human to create clever and image creative ability,but nowadays, robots invention that I believe it had had enough ability to help future human to raise more clever and more creating image or painting picture, art design etr. image ability, after robots had been experienced above more than ten years improvement stage from early research stage to invention stage, till to nowadays improvement stage, e.g. non-manual driving auto vehicels, even future non-manual driving skill may be improved to apply to public transport tools, e.g. trams, trains,buses, airplanes, ships etc. public transport tools, when non-manual driving skills can be improved to own the most safe driving skillful ability to compare human driving skills.

On another hand, when robots could be invented to be applied to medical or hospital surgery aspect, e.g. roboting surgerys may help surgery doctors to do complex surgery in surgery rooms, or serving patients tasks in any hospital working environments. They can help nurses and doctors to spend more time to do more important tasks urgently, so medical or surgery serving robots may help nurses and surgery doctors to reduce task load pressure and create clever or improve their surgery skills to when they can cooperate to work in hospitals.

On the other hand, robots can be invented to help any public transport drivers to avoid more traffic accidents occurrence on any countries roads. So, it seems that non-manual driving public transport tools invention may also help human drivers to improve driving skills in possible, when they can learn how to avoid sudden traffic accidents occurrence in any countries roads in any time. so, any kindsof public transport tool drivers ought learn how to avoid traffic accidents skills from future non-manual driving robots invention. Instead of non-manual driving robots and hospital patients medical care or surgery service robots may help public transport tools drivers and hospital nurses and doctors to concentrate on spending time to treat any more important and urgent matters every days. Even, future restaurants may let cooking restaurants may let cooking robots to help human cookers to cook more different kinds of good taste food, to human cookers may learn cooking robots cooking skills in order to improve themselves traditional cooking skills often, in order to compare their cooking skills between human cookers and cooking robots.

On conclusion, it seems that cooking robots ought help human cookers to create any kinds of new cooking skills. Moremove, futuer robot cookers ought be future human cookers their cooking coaches. These robot cookers will help human cookers to create clever cooking skills in possible. Also, future non-manual driving robots ought help human drivers to create new driving skills in order to improve their driving skills to reduce sudden traffic accidents occurrence easily on any countries roads in any time, future hospital surgery or patient care service robots may help surgeons or nurses to do any surgerys in surgery rooms or looking care patients in hospitals. So, when robot surgeons help human surgeons to do complex surgerys in surgerical rooms, human surgeons can learn how to do more complex surgerical tasks for every surgeons when human surgeons can observate every surgerical robots how to do surgeons together. Hence, it seems that robot surgeons also may create future human surgeons themselves innovate surgerical skills from traditional surgerical skills improvement. So, future artificial intelligent technology ought help any kinds of human occupations to create clever, even improvement themselves traditional skills to new innovative skills absolutely.

Why does technology raise online products sale demand and reduces shops products sale demand?

Nowadays robot technology is popular to be applied to different aspects of our daily lives. They may include: non-manual driving vehicles, smart phones, space rockets, kitchen cookers, shopping centres service, cinema ticket sale, etc. different kinds of businesses demand. However, instead of internet invention may influence global communication, media channel is changed to computer internet, media channel is changed to computer internet, media communication from traditional newspaper, letter, TV, radio etc. communication channel. So, any internet users may click to yahoo.com news website to read global news from computer yahoo.com website easily.

In fact, internet technology is also used from businesses. They attempt to set up themselves web stores to sell their products from themselves webstores. So, any one product buyers may buy any kinds of products from any one webstores when they stay at homes. It is very convenient and common to future any one webstore shoppers. It brings this question: Can webstores help online product purchases needs raise and influence shop product purchases need reduce?

In demand and supply view, when one product price raises, its sale demand ought reduce, unless, it can attract to influence customers need consideration or its supply number decreases. But, when one product is increasing sale price to seel from the seller's webstore, whether its sale number will be influenced to reduce. Also, when the kind of product is selling and its sale price is raised, whether it can still keep demand number increase as well as whether it can influence its similar kinds of competitor their products sale demand number to reduce from shop sale channel.

In demand and supply view, when one product price raises, its sale demand ought reduce, unless, it can attract to influence customers need consideration or its supply number decreases. But when one product is increasing sale price to sell from the seller's webstore, whether its sale number will be influenced to reduce. Also, when the kind of product is selling and its sale price is raised, whether it can still keep demand number increases as well as whether it can influence its similar kinds of competitors their products sale demand number to reduce from shop sale channel.

I suppose that webstore sale may influence shop sale demand number decreases, because when internet is popular to use, when one country's buyer wants to buy one kind of product, but he/she can not find the kind of product can be bought from himself/herself home country. If he/she can findthe kind of product to buy from any one of overseas webstore from internet channel at home in any time. Then, he/she will be influenced to make purchase decision from the seller's websote immediately. So, it implies that when on consumer plans to buy one kind of product, he / she will attempt to find the kind of product from any one seller's webstore in preferat home, if he/she spend long time to find the kind of product from many of webstores, but he /she still does not find the kind of product from many of webstores, then he/she will choose to visit any one shop to attempt to buy the kind of product.Hence, online shopping purchase channel will be prefer choice to compare visiting shopd purchase channel in nowadays society.

So, it explains that why the kind of product online sale number may influence the kind of similar product visiting shop sale number either increases or decreases. It means that the kind of product visiting shops sale number may still increases , if the kind of similar products supply number is not enough , they are difficult to let any one online buyer to find to buy from any one webstore. Otherwise, if the kind of similar products sale supply number is enough to let any one online buyer to find from many webstores. Then, they can influence the similar kinds of shop products purchase demand to reduce and their shops purchase demand will be also influenced to reduce from webstores purchase channel.

On conclusion, it explains that the kind of shop products demand number ought be influenced to increase or decrease, when the similar kind of products can be bought easily from many webstores from internet (ecommerce) shopping channel. Internet (online) technology may help the seller to raise the kind of product competitive ability on purchase demand aspect, when there are not many other sellers can provide webstores to sell the similar kind of products and they only concentrate on selling the kind of similar products from shops to let any one online buyer to frind from may webstores. Then, they can influence the similar kinds of shop products purchase demand to reduce and their shops purchase demand will be also influenced to reduce from webstores purchase channel. Hence, webstore and shop both purchase channel explains that the similar kinds of shop products demand number will be influenced to increase or decrease , when the kinds of product can be bought easily from many webstores from internet shopping channel. Internet technology may help the seller to raise the kind of product competitive abilty to raise purchase demand when there are not many other sellers can provide webstores to sell the kind of similar products and they only concentrate on selling the kind of similar products from shops.

Does car technological development reach mature stage to help economic development?
Our societies had been developing too many years. In our past technological aspect, machine invention had began till to computer invention till to internet invention. It seems that our technological development stage may reach mature stage. Why do I feel our technological development had reached mature stage. I shall apply demand and supply economic theory to explain this question as below:
I shall indicate car development industry to explain whether when car development stage can reach mature stage, it may help global economic growth. In our car technological development stage, it is from gas energy car invention till to nowadays battery energy car invention till to even future non-manual driving car invention. Do you feel that when human (car buyers) felt environmental protecion need to avoid air pollution. So, battery energy cars demand number may increase , it will influence gas energy cars demand number reduces. Even, if future non0manula driving cars invention succeed, lazy driving car buyers will choose to buy non-manual driving (robot driving cars) in preference. So, it is possible that , it will influence future gas energy cars demand number reduces much. I mean that when car buyers can choose many different kinds of non-manual driving cars and battery energy cars to buy. Then, gas energy cars demand number must be

influenced to reduce very much as well as gas energy cars supply number will be influenced to reduce to avoid sale prices reduce.

Hence, it explains why future car technological development will reach mature stage when both kinds of non-manual driving cars and battery energy cars are invented to the mature stage. When these two kinds of cars invention can satisfy future global car buyers driving needs. Then, car maufacturers won't need to spend too much time to continue to attempt to invent any new kinds of cars in order to excite future car buyers' purchase decision. So, I believe that car technological development will reach mature stage within five years, if non-manual driving cars and battery energy cars are invented in success and they can be popular to accept to drive to global car buyers.

On conclusion, when car technological development reaches matural stage, it will help future economy continue grows because when car manufacturers had invented many new kinds of non-manual driving cars and new kinds of non-manual driving cars and new battery energy car sale market. Then, they will encourage or attract global many car buyers choose to buy these both kinds of cars products in preference to compare to traditional gas energy car products. So, they will influence many traditional gas- energy car buyers forgive to drive gas energy cars to avoid non pollution and lazy driving behavioral feeling. So, gas energy car reselling number will increase between gas energy car drivers and past non-owning any car buyers. Also, non-manual driving cars and battery energy car supplying number will be influenced to increase when battery energy car buyers and non-manual driving car buyers driving needs increase.

Consequently, these factors will influence global gas energy cars, non-manual driving cars and battery energy cars their cars purchase and sale transactions increase in future global car market. So, I believe that global car technological development could reach matural stage, then it will infuence global car buyers number increases as well as this car technological mature development stage may also bring global rapid economic growth future non-manual driving car buyers and battery energy car buyers both number increases.